The World According to Coleen

Coleen Grissom

The World According to Coleen

To Lee — with every good wish — Coleen Grissom

Trinity University Press | SAN ANTONIO

Published by Trinity University Press
San Antonio, Texas 78212
Copyright © 2015 by Coleen Grissom

Cover design by Sarah Cooper
Book design by DigiTek Publishing, Chennai, India

Trinity University Press strives to produce its books using
methods and materials in an environmentally sensitive manner.
We favor working with manufacturers that practice sustainable
management of all natural resources, produce paper using
recycled stock, and manage forests with the best possible
practices for people, biodiversity, and sustainability. The press
is a member of the Green Press Initiative, a nonprofit program
dedicated to supporting publishers in their efforts to reduce
their impacts on endangered forests, climate change, and forest-
dependent communities.

The paper used in this publication meets the minimum
requirements of the American National Standard for
Information Sciences—Permanence of Paper for Printed Library
Materials, ANSI 39.48–1992.

978-1-59534-667-4 (paperback)
978-1-59534-668-1 (ebook)

CIP data on file at the Library of Congress

19 18 17 16 15 | 5 4 3 2 1

Contents

ix   *Introduction*

**Admonishing and Challenging Trinity
University Students**

3   *A Time for Growth*

5   *Memories*

9   *New Term*

12   *Student Complaints*

15   *End of Fall Semester*

19   *Fall Renewal*

22   *Vandalism*

26   *GPA*

29   *Racism circa 1978 at Trinity*

32   *Liberal Arts*

35   *Advice for Visiting Parents*

38   *Getting to Know One Another*

42   *Habits of Thriving Students*

45   *Life after Graduation*

48   *Graduation*

50   *Getting Ready for the Real World*

54   *Hope Chest*

Alumni

61   *Alumni Come Home*

63   *Alumni Weekend and All Its "Pleasures"*

66 *Avoiding Nostalgia*

71 *Alums*

Rare Travels and Unseemly Adventures

77 *Colorado Rockies*

80 *Fear of Flying*

84 *Trip to the Spa*

Fetishes and Compulsions

89 *Dieting*

92 *Collecting Moments*

96 *Keeping a Daily Journal*

102 *On Giving and Getting*

105 *Being Kind*

Some of My Favorite Things

111 *Thanksgiving*

114 *The Oscars*

118 *The Magic of Movies*

129 *Hero Worship and Role Models*

134 *Sacraments*

137 *Awards Programs*

141 *What You Most Love to Do*

Life Choices and Challenges

147 *The Small Stuff*

152 *"Companion" Animals*

163 *Resourcefulness and Perseverance*

166 *In Defense of Solitude*

170 *The Art of Fine Dining*

176 *Getting the Girl Out of East Texas*

181 *Dealing with Change*

Aging at Warp Speed

189   *Technology*

191   *Technology's Creeping Up on Me*

196   *Change*

199   *Clichés*

202   *I've Been Sick*

205   *The First Amendment*

211   *On the Cusp of My Dotage*

Introduction

Once upon a time, as I pondered the possibility that Trinity University Press would publish another collection of some of my writings following the successful 2008 sampling of my speeches, *A Novel Approach to Life*, I decided the writing I do perhaps even more than speeches was lists. So I began compiling examples of those as well as the column I've occasionally written for the student-edited newspaper, the *Trinitonian*, through the more than five decades that I've worked at Trinity.

Not surprisingly, neither lists nor columns made much sense out of context, fascinating (to me, at least) and timely as they were. So with the expert guidance of Trinity University Press director and editor, Barbara Ras, I've worked to expand and to update those pieces into meaningful essays.

This project, no surprise to anyone who knows me, results in an evolving collection of my views and opinions about all sorts of matters—reading, teaching, eating, living alone, traveling, viewing, pet caring, hero worshipping, whining, irritating, wheeling and dealing, surviving and thriving, and more—indeed, a sort of *The World According to Coleen* compilation.

Pick and choose—scan—rip pages out—write your own essays. Just know that whatever your reaction, I don't really care a lot. First of all, I'll probably never know. Also, compiling, elaborating upon, and categorizing this material was great fun. Shameless though it is, I can (and do) reread many of them and laugh so loud that I make the poodles bark and the cats run for cover, or I reread some and get so angry in recollecting the situation that outraged me then and now that I have to take a break and cheer up by watching an episode of something like *Dexter*. And, of course, rereading others makes me so sad at a recollected loss that I weep.

I hope that some of what follows will affect you a bit—maybe even make you laugh, frown, or cry—as it did me. After all, 2014 was the year of my eightieth birthday. Since I've always been so restrained and circumspect about my views, opinions, stances, and perspectives, surely it's about time I show less restraint and aim for candor and authenticity—sort of, saying what I mean and meaning what I say.

I hear tell (East Texas colloquialism) that people tend to repeat themselves as they age. As I proofread this manuscript, it occurred to me that I must have developed this quality early. Favorite quotations, anecdotes, and opinions reappear in this book. Please remind yourself that I wrote these essays over several decades and try not to be distressed by these occasional repetitions. Just focus on how well chosen they are, don't bother to point them out to me, and get on with your life.

Let's begin with a short history of my love of lists, since that's the focus which originally guided this writing project.

For as long as I can remember, I've been a list maker, and, as my compulsive behaviors set in with aging, I seem to list almost everything. Because listing engages, challenges, and amuses me, I hope readers will be motivated to make some of their own.

Have I convinced you that listing is fun? That it helps one be organized and avoid redundancy and backtracking? That it forces you (well, me, for sure) to focus on the blessings of life—not just annually in November, but every single day? Well, I certainly hope so, because you have in your hands my comments on lists which reveal aspects of life that I think matter.

Two lists—let's call them rituals rather than compulsions—that I compose regularly are, first, a list of "10 Things I Love to Do," which originated with a values clarification strategy decades ago, and which I now, ritualistically, create on January 1 annually. I find scanning these lists through the years tells me sometimes more than I want to know about ways I've changed and ways I've stayed the same.

Second, as I mention just about every time I get near a microphone, I make a list at the end of my day as I jot down "happiest times" to close my journal entry. Again, it's fun to reread these, especially to observe the gradual evolution from "hearing Tina Turner in concert" to "all clear reports on colonoscopy."

Thinking about "happiest times" just before sleep seems so much more conducive to pleasant dreams than recalling the list of horrific, violent deaths I've observed that evening on *Dexter*, *Criminal Minds*, and *Law & Order: SVU*.

Those are my only two compulsive/ritualistic lists, but I have many others that are "usual," and many of them proved to be excellent fodder for personal essays offering my views and opinions. For example, I keep a running list of errands and arrange them by location, making sure not to backtrack. "Mail letters at post office" must precede "get cash from ATM" and "pick up meds at Walgreens."

For grocery shopping, I take a similar, but more complicated, approach: since I jot down items as I realize I need them, the order of the needs is haphazard and disorganized. Thus, before going to HEB, I number the items in order of their location in the store—again, avoiding backtracking. (The location of the frozen foods section with Blue Bell "Light" Vanilla near the cashiers' checkout aisles at the front of store presents a challenge, but I cope.)

On weekends during the academic year, I prepare for teaching my classes, and list making abounds! What do I want to accomplish? How can I avoid repetition? How can I stay focused? How do I prevent the smart-aleck sophomore from pulling me off subject? How can I make sure the shy student who wants to enter the discussion has opportunities to do so? I achieve all this most of the time by working from notes I prepare and type—big 14-point, double-spaced notes—for each class, even inserting various students' names to assure I call on them.

In those semesters in which I teach two sections of the same course, having carefully prepared notes/lists for *each* class is essential. What could be more humiliating than realizing halfway through some pontification that I had already covered that in this very same section, probably just a few minutes ago? "Prepare clear, organized notes for teaching"—write that down.

In writing speeches, though I struggle to offer fresh observations, I have most assuredly grown repetitive through the years. The tradition I follow of closing speeches with a sampling of quotations from my reading that guides my life helps me present some new material with each speech, as well as repeating and reemphasizing longtime favorites. At the end of my annual newsletter, I close with a new quotation from my reading that particular year, hoping the words will be provocative, motivational, and even moving.

Have I convinced you that in this collection of essays I'm going to be forthright and straightforward? No longer aiming for subtlety and evasiveness? I hope so, because readers who vigorously disagree with my views and opinions might want to follow Bette Davis's advice: "Fasten your seatbelts, it's going to be a bumpy night!"

Admonishing and Challenging
Trinity University Students

A Time for Growth

When I agreed in the summer to write a column for the *Trinitonian*, it seemed like a swell idea, for, as Erin said, "It'll give the students a chance to know you as a person." (If not "as a person," I shudder to think what they might think of me as.) Dare I reveal more than you already heard during orientation from supportive colleagues, enthusiastic, "Grissomized" staff, and jaded upperclassmen?

Why not risk it? Let me share some thoughts: The distinguished British actor Charles Laughton observed in an introduction to the anthology *Tell Me a Story* that he felt regret whenever he entered a library because he realized that in one short lifetime he could never read all those books. This observation which moved me so much when I first read it many years ago came vividly to mind Sunday night when John Narciso reminded us to watch TV's *Supermarket Sweepstakes*, a contest in which the participants in a timed period grabbed up all they could from the grocery shelves. John compared this to the opportunity afforded to students in college.

So that's the topic foremost in my mind these past few days: how to motivate new students—and even possibly shake a few returning ones out of their lethargy—

and urge all to use the occasion of the college experience to live richly, to investigate widely, to take all they can get from the myriad of opportunities available to them at Trinity. Already I've heard echoing off the walls of the Coates Center such phrases as "I have to take science," "I don't know anything about computers. How can I pass C&IS 308?" and "My adviser ignored the fact that I've always gone to Sunday school and scheduled me for Medieval Studies." Why do some choose a liberal arts school, then resist every chance to become more liberalized?

I thought about this only a few days before orientation. I had told a friend that I had spent a boring evening ironing clothes so that I wouldn't have to wear the same dress throughout orientation week, and she had responded, "You iron? What are you—a Renaissance woman?" Far from it, unfortunately, but I am a woman who welcomes the explosion of knowledge, the rich backgrounds and varied expertise of my colleagues, who stumbles through books about subjects I'll never understand, who forces herself to see a wide spectrum of films even if some are X-rated and necessitate wearing sunglasses and a trench coat to guarantee anonymity.

Like Charles Laughton, I can't bear the awareness that I just won't have time to read all the books, to talk with all the professors, to get to know all the students, but I can at least say that I'll give it a good try and urge my students to consider the same.

The brevity of your lifespan on this campus and the abundance of opportunities for growth—how will you reconcile these?

Memories

To fans of my column over the years: do not rejoice prematurely. I'm only going to write an occasional column. The new *Trinitonian* staff wants to offer the column opportunity to a wider range of administration, faculty, and staff.

To those repulsed by my column over the years: rejoice. See above.

I write this column for the year's initial issue under some duress. It's Labor Day weekend. The sky is blue and the sun is warm. And, frankly, I'd rather be somewhere outside inviting the solar rays that, when you are younger than I, supposedly prematurely wrinkle the skin. Surely my age group is safe from such admonitions since we are wrinkled already.

Grudgingly I scrawl some thoughts to share with you:

It's the start of another academic year at Trinity. If I calculate correctly, and I don't always, it's the twenty-first fall semester I've worked on this campus. About as many years as the members of the senior class have been alive. Career mobility has never been my thing.

So I reflect today on what, from my perspective, Trinity has been, what it has become, and what it ultimately will be.

When I arrived—in a red Nash Rambler, not a covered wagon—as a twenty-four-year-old head resident, I entered and responded gratefully to a truly personalized institution. President Jim Laurie knew everyone by name—from maids to deans. (There were neither custodians nor vice presidents in those days. Ah, the price of progress!) I emulated him, knew all the women residents of Myrtle, Isabel, and Susanna (that's all the "girls' dorms" there were) by name, and the maids, specifically Florence Huff and Ruby Hunter, were my friends.

Kind, elderly, retired gentlemen comprised the "security force" and were great favorites with the "girls," for they frequently boosted late returnees over the balconies when they sneaked into the dorms at 8:45 p.m., after curfew. A woman named Blanche King was the food service, and I always suspected that she personally tested every morsel served.

In those early days there were concerts in the Sams Center with The Association or Peter, Paul, and Mary; registration was, alas, primevally done by hand; lines were short, bills were itemized correctly, and we all knew who had signed up for our classes by the first day they met.

I wore an ash blonde bouffant hairdo and looked swell on Tuesdays when I left the Radiant Lady beauty parlor. The rest of the week, once the spray net melted, my hairdo was the pits.

Later Trinity aspired to become the "Princeton of the Southwest." We "Simon Pured" sports and built up tennis. We constructed attractive yet less homey residence halls. The bookstore, paradoxically, began to sell T-shirts advertising Trinity as a country club. In those days we had a few streakers, a couple of panty raids, and a candlelight vigil on the evening of the massacre at Kent State.

Additional red brick buildings appeared as if overnight. Beloved colleagues grew older, retired, or died; a few moved on to bigger and better things. I, like so many of my colleagues, despaired over some changes, rejoiced over others, but never really thought seriously of leaving.

If you are a decent sort, surely you are asking, "What's kept her here?" Or, less charmingly, "Won't she ever go—except feet first?"

I've stayed so long partly out of a limited vision of the possibilities of personal achievement—educated women of my age group in the South have not exactly reaped the full benefits of affirmative action. I've stayed because I love this part of the country and its peace. But mostly I've stayed these past twenty years and never made any serious attempt to investigate other administrative positions because I believe in commitment, and I made two decades ago and have reaffirmed frequently a commitment to the fundamental philosophy of this institution—to provide a quality liberal arts education to young persons capable of responding to it in a well-maintained, aesthetically satisfying environment where mutual respect, tolerance, and trust dominate.

This philosophy has been shaky some days; to some, it seems a wee bit shaky now. But I've been here too long and seen too much to join with those who bemoan that we are heading to hell (Editor: Should I write "the lower regions" in the interest of good taste?) in a handbasket.

What this institution is transcends. The heart, the pulse—ah, how poetic—of this place does not change. Those of us who are committed to Trinity see the quest for what it stands for in the eyes of the new students—in their vulnerable, open desire to be loved, respected, trusted, challenged.

So rejoice all of you that I will write rare columns, for I am most assuredly in one of my didactic eras! Do not despair. Do not gripe. Do not badmouth. Teach excitingly. Administer judiciously and efficiently. Do what you say you'll do. Go out of your way to be kind. Help one another.

Remember where we've been, and, by your actions and your commitment, ensure where we're going.

New Term

Here I go again, sharing what's on my short list of concerns in a bimonthly column for my favorite newspaper at my favorite university. I seem never to grasp that elusive skill of saying no.

The fall semester's behind us and the spring well under way, so I am girding up my loins to cope with the inevitable student complaints about my classes. Happily the "class climate evaluations" continue to be positive, even occasionally hyperbolically generous, but there are two recurrent complaints: first, she makes us read too much. (I ignore that one; what could my students possibly be doing with their time that could be more valuable—even enjoyable—than reading superb contemporary fiction? That my students do anything other than focus on my course baffles me as to their priorities.)

The second inevitable complaint, which I will rephrase with my usual discreet censorship, goes something like this: the books are "too dark."

Apparently, my current students grew up reading the same books I did. Those texts almost always ended with some variant of these satisfying, albeit vague, words: "And they lived happily ever after." Humbug.

I don't teach novels with those endings. Last fall I did attempt one "romance novel" in my 2308 class, but I was so nauseated throughout the teaching and the leading of discussion that I dumped the sucker from this term's readings. My health was suffering.

Each semester, in a so far futile effort to discourage students from whining about "dark" stories, I read aloud the marvelous Margaret Atwood's succinct essay "Happy Endings," which you can find readily online. She elucidates plotting in fiction and in "real life" (i.e., "John and Mary die").

The students ignore this wisdom, but I persevere, and when the 2013 winner of the Nobel Prize for Literature, Alice Munro, appeared last week on NPR's streamed program *Symphony Space* in conversation with her friend Margaret Atwood, these two literary geniuses addressed my topic.

Atwood questioned Munro about readers' complaints that Munro's character were "too mean or bad." The Nobel Laureate responded, "Has anybody ever written a book that was really good with people who were nice all the time, or even part of the time?" I hollered at my computer screen, "My students are desperately seeking that book."

It gets better: Munro acknowledged complaints about her "less-than-sunny plots" and readers wanting to read books that "make them feel good, make them feel happy." (These *are* my students!) But Munro admitted that she couldn't write such novels, partly because her favorite books were those such as *Wuthering Heights*. Then she stated (as I will henceforth also state), "I didn't understand that you read books in order to feel that the world is better than it is, and so I was offending without really understanding it for quite a while."

I select the required readings for my classes primarily because of the superiority of the writing, but I also read, recommend, and require texts that, I think, achieve verisimilitude in the depiction of "real" life—ones that capture the joys and triumphs of life as well as the sorrows and losses.

Most significantly, I prefer readings that do not try to trick me into seeing the world as better than it is, but ones that remind me of what really matters, what makes a positive difference, and challenges me (and my recalcitrant students) to work hard to "become all that you were created capable of being," as Carlyle put it.

It is my humble view that a Trinity education should help one do that; I welcome a new semester and another opportunity to move toward that goal.

Student Complaints

I planned a Spring Break theme for this column—using quotes such as Earl Wilson's "A vacation is what you take when you can no longer take what you've been taking." But when I realized that the phrase "been taking" might refer to my classes or those of my peers, I decided to eschew such a potentially disturbing topic.

Helpfully, a woman in one of those very classes said recently, "You used to be vice president for student affairs, didn't you?" After glancing around furtively to see if this was some sort of trap, I admitted that I had served for several decades in that division. This student, as Trinity undergraduates usually do, had a follow-up question: "Why do we have to live on campus?"

I, shamefully, don't know or wish to know much about current campus policies that apply outside the classroom, and I'm certainly unfamiliar with the language used these days to explain and/or to defend policies unpopular with some. Nevertheless, I do have experience and opinions on this topic, and here's a summary:

When I first came to work here, there were 144 resident "girls" who lived in the McFarlin Complex; the "boys" lived elsewhere and wherever, including Grande Courts, but let's not go there, literally or in any other sense of the phrase.

There were other students who lived in the city with their families; these "townies" expressed that attending Trinity was "just like high school," and certainly it must have been for them. They commuted, ate separately in the Student Union Building coffee shop, and only rarely got involved in campus activities. They felt (sadly and accurately) that they were "second-class citizens."

As those in positions of authority engaged in long-range planning, we wanted to include all students in the life of this campus; we wanted to create a true academic community. Thanks to generous donors, the capacity for student housing increased with "dorms" and services about which everyone bragged—maid service, no group showers and toilets down the hall, spacious storage, and, luxury of luxuries—private balconies. (Don't get me started on ways those balconies were a bane of my early years here; girls checked in at the 8:30 curfew, then promptly sneaked out over the balconies. Good old days? I don't think so.)

In creating this community we desired, among other goals, to meet students' basic needs—services providing not only comfortable housing but also food, health care, athletic activities, research opportunities (libraries and labs). We hoped to enable students to focus on their education both in and outside the classrooms, acquiring knowledge and polishing skills that would serve them well throughout their lives.

Predictably, students never appreciated these as much as some felt they should: one would get the "roommate from hell" and be miserable, another would resent some health service policy, but the perennial target of most complaints was and remains the food service—prices, quality, hours of operation.

When we provided only one entrée served cafeteria style for limited hours, some hated it. When we had a "women's dining hall" with waiters serving the meal, students complied with a certain dress code and stood until I tapped my water glass, and we all sang the doxology; some hated that.

And today, just as then, some of you forcefully state: I want to cook my own meals. Well, I "cook" mine by picking them up at Central Market or Whole Foods and heading for the microwave. My younger colleagues with families somehow make time to shop for fresh produce and fixin's after or between classes, with children in tow or waiting supper at home. I think if you ask those who do cook how they find the time or energy to do so, their answer wouldn't be enviable.

Here's the student life dean still lurking in me: Celebrate the opportunities and appreciate the services that Trinity provides. As have most who preceded you here, develop lifelong friendships. When you gather for reunions, appreciate the irony as you gripe about your memories of the food and the residency policy even as you reminisce about your years at this remarkable community that so enriched your life.

End of Fall Semester

Although I honestly cannot imagine that anyone other than the dedicated proofreaders at the *Trinitonian* will be reading this or much else outside of class assignments at this season of the academic year, I see by my trusty calendar that the due date for my third short list of the semester approaches. Since I try never to miss a deadline, here I am composing like crazy instead of grading three stacks of fat, fascinating essays.

Don't jump to the conclusion that writing is more fun than grading. It's truly a toss-up.

In pre-Thanksgiving class sessions, it distressed me to note that my students appeared exhausted and depleted. In writing workshop we even had a disturbingly candid discussion about the amount of sleep and exercise the students were getting at this hectic time of the semester. Is it news to anyone but me that the students are missing exercise because they've decided that thirty more minutes of sleep is the greater need? Or that no one admitted that he or she felt prepared for end-of-term projects and tests?

Maybe the Thanksgiving break helped. Maybe most will return revived by good home-cooked meals, touch football with relatives, or sleeping late. But then they face the throes of finishing out the term, and, in my experience, rest, exercise, and nutritious meals don't carry over much. Nevertheless, we must attend to these physical needs before we can cope with the final stretch, which demands endurance, discipline, and focus.

So on my short list is urging that you realize you are—big surprise—merely human. Make getting some exercise, some sleep, and some healthy food high priorities as we enter the end-of-semester marathon.

I realize there are zillions of distractions, including my least favorite—the repugnant commercialization of some of the most holy seasons of the year. Much to my dismay, as I drove to campus on Thursday, November 17, I discovered that one of my oldies-but-goodies radio stations had already switched to music of the season—you know, "I Saw Mommy Kissing Santa Claus" and Muzak versions of "O Holy Night." I almost drove off into the median.

In this dreadful economy, you'd think I would approve the early openings of stores for Black Friday and the myriad of obnoxious ads (the one I most abhor features that ridiculously excited woman in "Santa Claus red" preparing herself for shopping at Target by heavy lifting and sprinting.) Yet again, the message of the season, it seems, is spend, spend, spend.

To be fair, I also see coverage (limited, but existing) of acts of compassion: providing food for holiday meals, inviting military personnel to dinners in "real" homes, rescuing beagles from labs and introducing them to freedom and to loving homes.

But there never seems to be enough emphasis on what I believe should be the focus of this season—even as students struggle with completing end-of-term exams and projects and my colleagues and I struggle with grading them.

It will surprise no one who knows me that one of my mottos is "Happiness is wanting what you have," and that I direct friends and family to give me no more ceramic poodles, fine wine in boxes, cat teasers, or new novels I "really must read." I ask those with whom I exchange gifts to tell me their favorite charities and nonprofits, and much as they might hope for a gift certificate for the New Braunfels Smokehouse or Coldwater Creek, they mutter, "You know how she is" and pretend to be pleased that I've donated in their honor to their church or to a nonprofit they support.

As for me, much as they would like to add scented candles to my décor, they comply and send checks to what I admire and support: Trinity University Press, Gemini Ink, the Cibolo Nature Center, the Hill Country Animal League, the Trinity scholarship established by the Alumni Association in my name.

Few of us need more things. So on my short list, in response to the urge to spend and buy, is this: consider this year *not* shopping online or standing in line pushing, shoving, or even squirting competitors with pepper spray to buy slightly lower-priced electronic toys. Instead, realize that if ever there is a season in which we should "do good," this is it.

If you must rationalize this approach, memorize one or both of these wise observations: William James's "Act as if what you do makes a difference. It does," or, probably better, Dr. Seuss's "Unless someone like you cares a whole awful lot, nothing is going to get better. It's not."

During these holidays—this semester break—rejuvenate yourself and make a positive difference through your choices.

Fall Renewal

You didn't understand. Last week "Reflections" concerned my midlife crisis, and the amusing bouffant hairdo photo was my idea. Illustrating vanished youth, don't you see? So there's really no need for me to sue the *Trinitonian*.

Spending most of my week defending my selection of a photo with a wrinkle-free countenance and unfrosted hair left little time for reflection for this issue. Should I write of San Antonio rain and drainage systems? Both are so bad that students from my classes did call the office anonymously on Wednesday to ask—in futile hope of a negative response—"Was she able to get to the office today?" She was, class met, people flunked, people passed; so it goes.

Should I write of the initial sessions of our Student Development classes? It would probably be premature to tell much, but the enrollment is primarily freshmen/sophomores; there is remarkable candor and openness about first impressions of TU and the "college experience"; there is an eagerness to get all they can from their years here; and there's an invigorating commitment to learning more about themselves. With this start, how can these classes fail to be worthwhile?

No, I'll leave dealing with the rain to Ashmore, Dawson, and Maclovio, and I'll postpone reflecting on the S.D. classes for a few weeks; what I want to share this week may be hackneyed, but I think we ought to note it:

Everywhere in our country as summer ends and fall begins, people seem to write the season off as dull, unrewarding, transitional, relieved only by gobbling huge Thanksgiving dinners, cheering for the Cowboys, and raking leaves. Even the movies in this city are the dregs— who cares about the diet of piranhas, bug-eyed Feldman's attempts to "think dirty," or having their ears gratuitously pierced by Dunaway's screams as Ms. Mars? Whatever happened to classics such as *Benji*, *Love Story*, and *You Light Up My Life*? Now, in 1978, we find the city's theaters are without relief except for the tasteless and hilarious *Animal House*, which, by the way, is no satire. Some of us were there. That's stark realism if ever I've seen it. But in the field of education there is an absence of this dullness because, for us, fall is the season of rebirth, renewal.

I've heard Bruce Thomas say that no other business affords an opportunity to start all over again every year. We're granted a fresh chance to avoid past mistakes, to make deeper commitments, to be more caring, to be better prepared for class and/or administrative responsibilities; to wit, to clean up our act. As I read the *Trinitonian* last week, I wondered how many of us are tempted to wait until "new leadership comes to Trinity" to put forth our best. New leadership will get here "in its own good time," as we say in the piney woods. Meanwhile, this is the only first fall semester of college for over six hundred freshmen and, I suspect, a rather significant fall term for most of our returning students. Surely, the commitment of this institution is to the future, but I hope we won't forget our responsibility to the present and casually overlook this particular season of renewal and rebirth.

Vandalism

A university is a community of scholars, and a university is a community where rational conduct and respect for others is normal behavior. Too much of my energy lately has been directed toward dealing with incidents that negate these definitions. And, because of the destructive actions of a few, I've had some trouble convincing others that this is, indeed, a university. Sometimes I've even forgotten.

You knew I'd have to address the issue of vandalism this week. I will, but I'll refrain from giving a defense of how our most recent case was handled. Why not focus on the real issue in this case, the vandals? Will you believe they threatened other students who observed their actions? Will you believe that, after all the clamor over the injustice of charging the hosts of the party for the damage, the vandals themselves have not come forward?

How does it feel, I wonder, to let someone else accept the financial and ethical responsibilities for your actions?

The issue is vandalism and theft on this campus. Do you have any idea how much university property is stolen or destroyed each year? How many apartments are furnished with Coates Center, Murchison Lounge, Laurie

Auditorium furniture? Assistant Residential Adviser Slater estimates a loss of $1,455 already this fall, and you wonder why their entrée can sometimes be described as "MM," or mystery meat? Did you know that someone deliberately destroyed the mechanism on both the Thomas and Lightner elevators last April and that repair costs totaled over $7,000? (In case of future vandalism of the elevators, we've already decided we just won't repair them. That'll be convenient for and fair to the Thomas-Lightner residents.) And I guess I should apologize for a sexist statement, but I honestly don't believe many of the vandals are women. Thieves of dishes and utensils, maybe, but "ripper-outers" of exit signs and destroyers of elevators, not likely.

How can we stop—or at least markedly decrease— the amount of theft and vandalism on this campus? I know several pretty effective steps we can take. Some wouldn't even cost any money; some would.

Without any financial investment, we could revoke the students' privilege of having beer and wine on campus. Without any financial investment, we could revoke the students' privilege of entertaining guests of the opposite sex in their rooms certain hours each day. Without any financial investment, we could end relocation, put all women back on the west campus, all men on the east, and return to the system of permitting guests only in the resident hall lounges and only a few hours each day.

Or, if we're willing to spend some money, we could decrease vandalism and theft by dropping the idea of RAs.

Instead of hiring "blow-off" seniors, we could hire more costly but more conscientious older adults who would more stringently enforce the few regulations we still have governing student conduct. Or, if we're willing to spend a little more money, we could employ staff to frisk students as they leave food service areas and to apprehend those walking out with a place setting for six. For a bit more money, we could increase the investment in Smith Security and have regular twenty-four hour patrols of each and every foot of the university property. And for even more money, we could build a wall around the campus, install gates for entrance and exits, and search all who come and go. We might stop some thefts and discourage a few of the creepy crawlers who flash around here now and then.

Each of these has some appeal; each has been considered as a possible reasonable step to take.

I want, however, to resist any action that would limit student rights or would result in penalizing the whole for the faults of the few. But the simple fact is that the security staff and the Student Affairs staff cannot be the only responsible persons on this campus, the only ones willing to get involved, to take a stand.

Too many Trinity University students turn the other way, tolerate any behavior, never stand up to any peers, no matter what rules they break or what inconvenience or expense they cause. (Who, by the way, do you think pays for replacement of broken ceiling tiles, ripped-out exit signs, or stolen knives and forks? Believe me, there's no rich donor's fund for this. Ultimately, you and yours absorb this expense.)

Do I sound cranky? I guess I do. I guess I am. It's been a rough fall. When Erin Baker (the paper's managing editor) asked me to share my reflections each week, little did she anticipate this kind of harangue. I so love my work, this university, you students, but in all candor, it's hard to defend some of you some of the time and fight for preservation of your right to be treated as adults.

GPA

It is hard for me to realize that both midsemester and homecoming have come and gone; it seems only a week or so ago that I was reading my "Keep Your Perspective" letter to an auditorium full of anxious freshmen. But now most of them are blasé campus sophisticates casually approaching the vicissitudes of preregistration with the aplomb of veterans. Nobody seems very anxious anymore. Most freshmen I talk with seem to possess an abundance of information on spring semester courses as well as on each faculty member's foibles and strengths. Supplementing our carefully evolved faculty advising system, quite a grapevine exists on this campus. There's no way to avoid this grapevine—and we probably shouldn't even if we could, but I do fret some days over how grade-conscious undergraduates have become.

Too many students I talk with care more about whether or not the instructor is an easy grader than about the focus of the course, and, when they plan for preregistration, the ease of the class and the convenience of the schedule seem to govern the decision-making process. Perhaps the tightness of the economy, the necessity that each graduate be marketable, and the high standards of admission for professional schools make this concern over grades inevitable, but it still distresses me. I don't even like it very much that young people have to determine by the time they are eighteen years old which professional schools they will attend! I hope most of you aren't avoiding meaty courses and demanding teachers just to keep up a high GPA.

Hey, I have a simple solution! Take lots of demanding courses, goof off less, spend a few more hours each day in study; work, as your parents and I relish saying, toward your "full potential"! Risk a few C's, but stretch yourself to your limit!

Because I have the privilege and the pleasure of teaching two courses this fall, I witness several times a week some stretching to the limits as well as some more leisurely approaching of learning. I love refereeing debates over where Jack London's narrator reveals that his sympathies are with the dog and not the man in the engrossing story "To Build a Fire," and I admire the ardor with which more advanced scholars dispute whether Hardy's Eustacia Vye threw herself or fell into the weir. Who wins these arguments isn't important; what is important is developing the skills of careful reading and of reasoned discourse in disputation.

I truly believe that all over this campus in dozens of classrooms many of our students are approaching their limits, and some of them are even having a good time doing it. If you're not one of these happy souls, why not just give it a try for the spring term or at least for a course or two this spring?

Your folks probably won't really disinherit you if you make a C, and you just might still have a chance for a full and useful life in spite of how influential a high GPA is reputed to be.

Racism circa 1978 at Trinity

At the Union in Austin last week I viewed the powerful Giuliano Montaldo film *Sacco and Vanzetti* and reflected for several days on this appalling case of prejudice and injustice.

Meanwhile, friends shared reactions of their viewing of a television program last week on the new Ku Klux Klan, and all of us educated, detached souls felt relieved that the Sacco-Vanzetti horror is just a footnote in the history of the 1920s and that the KKK, if it really still exists at all, functions in unenlightened, backwoodsy areas.

But just imagine that here at Trinity, your telephone rings, and you rush to answer it, assuming it's a friend offering some timely idea for a study break, but instead, it's an anonymous caller who addresses you by a derogatory phrase for your race and threatens, "We're going to get rid of you." Off you bop toward your room, your refuge from the tribulations of a hard day as a college senior, and you stare at your door, where someone has written, in green spray paint, "KKK kills niggers."

Your whole lifestyle begins to change. You suddenly suspect that everyone with whom you associate, no matter what their color, is capable of racial harassment or personal aversion. Small occurrences such as the ringing of a telephone or a knock at the door now cause you to tense with apprehension.

Sound like something out of the 1920s, or '30s, or, at the very least, the backwoods?

Well, as most of you know, it's not. It's happening here and now in this church-related college, this community of scholars, this enlightened university in the sun. I don't wish to suggest that this is the first case of intimidation I've dealt with, but like all of them, it's certainly unsavory and predictable. Perpetrators of such acts are creepily persistent, sly, full of energy and possessing much leisure time which they choose to devote to agitating and distressing other human beings.

I can't find excuses to help rationalize or explain any such behavior whether it's directed toward a person whose skin is a different color, one whose faith you don't understand, one whose apparent sexual preference you find disgusting, or one whose moral standards are different from your own.

How I wish that my expression of my revulsion over such actions would inspire some of you to inform on the harassers, to have the guts to say to peers, "I, too, am revolted by what you're doing, and I'm willing to testify against you." But I couldn't even flush out a vandal, so I have no dreams of inspiring confession or testimony.

Heeding Voltaire, I cultivate my own garden, and I know my weaknesses. I am intolerant of intolerance, and I don't know how to respond to a mother of a black student who says to me, "I went through this, and I prayed my daughter wouldn't have to. But I do have dreams of what a society should be." It's all been said far better than I ever could by a great philosopher: "the society that is to be created, where individuals grow freely, and where hate and greed and envy die because there is nothing to nourish them."

If ever such a society could exist, wouldn't you think it'd have its best chance on a college campus? In the fall of 1978 at Trinity University, it certainly doesn't look very promising.

Liberal Arts

During my college years and until recently in my professional life, the burning question of undergraduates was "Am I marriageable?" (A few of us apparently were not, but we've managed to muddle through somehow.) But now all I hear is "Am I marketable?"

Orientation week offered a simulation of a faculty club conversation between scholars representing the humanities, business, and engineering debating this topic. Last week student leaders directed questions to the new president about Trinity's "responsibility" for "placing" its graduates in jobs. Even the headline for an essay in last week's *Chronicle of Higher Education* glared at me and demanded to know, "Are liberal arts graduates good for anything?"

If they are truly liberally educated, they ought to be. They ought to develop certain competencies—check your curriculum. Those who are marketable refine their skills in communicating clearly and assertively, then make some attempts to grasp something of the sciences, the humanities, music, art, literature. They use the four years of the undergraduate experience to prepare themselves so that when they are ready for a full-fledged career they'll be personable, thoughtful, self-assured, articulate individuals who are eminently trainable.

Case in point: Never having heard of marketability, I changed majors just about every time I saw a 1955 version of the basic data sheet. I loved and perversely declared as a major at some point each of the following: physical education, Spanish, history, English, biology. (And had environmental science, gerontology, computing science, solar engineering, or organizational communication been discovered in those ancient days, I surely would have declared them, too.)

Keeping my academic file correctly updated must have sorely challenged the administration, so the antics of some of you are my just deserts. You reap what you sow in this world, or so my mother always admonished me.

Because I could not seem to narrow my studies, I learned a little about several fields, and because I yearned for friends and adventure and became involved in extracurriculars, I developed a few leadership and public speaking skills. When the time for marketing came, I was, therefore, fairly self-confident, fairly well-rounded (in both a literal and figurative sense), and somewhat trainable.

No one needs to observe how much the world has changed in all these years; we all realize that. What I'm trying to say is that much has stayed the same. Unless you aim to be in the fields of medicine or engineering, your best investment as an undergraduate is the same now as it was then: Liberate yourself through the liberal arts and you'll appeal to almost any market.

John Stuart Mill wrote, "Men are men before they are lawyers or physicians or manufacturers; and if you make them capable and sensible men, they will make themselves capable and sensible lawyers and manufacturers." (Let's assume if he were writing today, he'd replace "men" with "persons.")

Let us help you try to become capable and sensible; that's the hard part. The rest is easy. (Or, as my cliché-oriented English 309 class would put it, "The rest is as easy as rolling off a log.")

Advice for Visiting Parents

I title this occasional column "The Short List" because I select my topic from some concern, interest, anxiety, opinion that's at the top of my concerns, interests, anxieties, and opinions at the time I write the piece. Unfortunately, absolutely nothing—other than my hope that many parents and siblings attend Fall Family Weekend and that they take the residential life students out for a few meals—occurs to me about this university event being celebrated right now.

No matter what efforts my administrative colleagues make, no matter how awful one's roommate, no matter how boring one's writing workshop or how difficult the chemistry class, the number one complaint of almost every first-year student I have ever talked with on this campus is some silly thing about the food. If parents haven't already heard that, they will.

I long ago trained myself to listen respectfully and try not to be dismissive of these gripes, but of course I, who go home to toss a "Smart Ones Three-Cheese Ziti Marinara" in the microwave, lack empathy on this topic. I do, however, remember quite well when Trinity students had plenty to complain about in dining services—only one cafeteria line, no special stations, rumors of "saltpeter" hidden* in every entrée, and an underlying assumption that everyone loves meatloaf, Salisbury Steak (aka mystery meat), and calves' liver. Though I deny being the author of the popular descriptive "Mabee meat, maybe Jell-o," I always thought it amusing, sometimes accurate, but not particularly witty.

So near the top of the sharable part of my short list here is some advice for visiting parents: Don't overreact to your child's complaints about the food. Reread the preceding paragraph, recall the campus food "back in the day," notice the barely visible hints of the beginning of the "freshman fifteen," and, still, host your child and her or his pals to a dinner off campus.

Beyond that counsel, I encourage parents to offer some encouragements about getting more sleep, developing time-management skills, attending classes, keeping up with the assignments, and taking advantage of the myriad of cultural and intellectual opportunities available on this campus and in this region. Probably your child will ignore you, but we on the faculty don't want to be the only ones, in a phrase from my East Texas childhood, "spitting into the wind."

---

* A widely believed urban legend is that this substance "reduced libido," which, without going into specifics, has never really been much of a problem with most Trinity undergraduates—a self-disciplined, mannerly lot.

I have never ascribed to the depressing cliché that "college is the best time of one's life," but I do believe it can be a unique time to expand one's horizons, explore opportunities, and, thanks to Trinity's uniquely gifted faculty and student body, form lifelong relationships that will enrich one's life. Taking advantage of this is what I really urge parents to encourage as they visit campus this weekend.

Getting to Know One Another

On those rare occasions when I have time to reflect and when my reflection is not particularly "heavy," as my students would say, one of the topics I focus on is the redundancy in my life of two aspects of Trinity student behavior: women students who transfer or crank away their time here because they never are late, and men students I reprimand who had a few too many beers when out with the guys and so lumber around the dorms wreaking havoc—or more precisely, wrecking fire extinguishers, wrecking windows, wrecking university property. Why, I have fretted for at least twenty years (I was a slow learner), don't these people go out together? It'd give the women male companionship, and, if they're lucky, stimulating conversation, and it'd alter the behavior of the men because of their desire to impress, protect, and entertain the women. Why, oh, why, I ask, aren't they out together?

Recently I've gotten conned by increasingly skilled undergraduates into working with something called SOUP (Social Opportunities Undiscovered but Possible), and these students are attempting to address the problems of social life at Trinity University with a controversial forum on February 7, 1980, which I've agreed to emcee. That this event will result in everyone's meeting the dream-mate of their choice I doubt, but perhaps it will thrust the long-whispered-about problem into the open and start us on the road to some concrete steps toward a solution. ("Concrete" road? Yellow brick road? Steps? Weird language.)

Although I've never been married, I have cherished close friendships with male friends, each of whom has added essential dimensions to my life. But when I was an undergraduate, I, like many of the Trinity students, lacked the self-confidence and the gutsiness to make the necessary efforts to meet men, and most of my close male friends have been friends in my older adult life. But I'm more selfish for my students than perhaps I was for myself those many years ago: whether the relationships you establish become romantic or intimate really isn't the point. The point is the added dimension I wish for you now.

In the old days I could explain why there was so little communication between the sexes on this campus: women lived in the west complex, men in the east; dining facilities were separate; there were no visitation hours; there was no relocation; there were always about two hundred more resident men, and the women were usually brighter and more mature.

None of this is true anymore, according to the data. I suspect the administration has done just about all it can do to make developing of friendships between the sexes possible. I suspect the institutional environment shouldn't be seen as the culprit anyway.

Why don't you get to know each other? Are the women snooty? Are the men bad dressers? Are the women too fast? Are the men too slow? Is there no place to go? Nothing to do? Or are these just hackneyed excuses for your lack of initiative? Or do none of you risk getting to know yourself and somebody else because it might make you look foolish? It's ironic to me that in this day bereft of restrictive social rules and mores we still conduct our male-female relationships as if it's 1955.

Why haven't all the popular psychology movements of the 1970s for learning to improve our relationships (t-groups, assertiveness training, Burkett's classes, sensitivity training) resulted in more spontaneous, more personally risky, and more personally rewarding behavior? What, for instance, keeps you from seeing an interesting-looking person, walking up, and saying, "I'd like to get to know you?" (Or can this only seem real in a song lyric?)

SOUP is an organized effort by some seriously concerned, intelligent, attractive young people to more clearly define the problem on this campus that results in socially unhappy men and women. It may well flop. One of my nightmares these days and nights is that the program on February 7 will be attended by 685 bright, concerned young women and by 6 junior men (sitting on the front row, no doubt) who are applying for RA. Lawsy, I hope not.

When it comes down to it, I don't care who among my students falls in love and lives happily ever after—so few manage that anyway these days—but I do sincerely want the collegiate experience at this institution to enrich, to broaden, to enliven. I want new dimensions added to the lives of the students with whom I work, new friendships formed, new self-assurances developed.

I'll be at SOUP's forum on February 7, very likely without a date. How about it? Won't you join me? You read interesting columns. You seem interesting. Maybe we can go and get a cup of coffee or stop at the library and study afterward.

Habits of Thriving Students

For as long as I can remember, I've loved lists—making them, checking them (more than twice), scratching off items accomplished (e.g., books read, chores done, groceries purchased, class preparations completed). I also delight in reading lists—for literary awards such as the Pulitzer, PEN/Faulkner, National Book, *New York Times*' Ten Best, Man Booker, Nobel—as well as less esoteric—the Grammys, Emmys, Tonys, Razzies, and, especially, Oscars.

Because of the compulsive nature of my relationship with lists, I've chosen the above title for this series of columns for my favorite undergraduate school newspaper for two reasons: first, among lists I regularly make is one of concerns, irritations, and anxieties, so I plan to compose these pieces around something that's been on my short list this month, preoccupying me. Second, I plan to write a book of lists to be published as a companion to *A Novel Approach to Life*, the collection of a sampling of my speeches from the past five decades, and maybe this will be a start on that project. You see, I'm not only compulsive, but also frugal and efficient, qualities I developed growing up and making the sacrifices necessitated by the Great Depression and World War II.

Certainly, my concerns as the summer of 2010 ends focus on the academic year, which, for me and my colleagues, offers yet again a fresh start, a chance to do things better, to avoid repeating mistakes, to make fewer new ones, to get it right this time. Even higher on my current concern lists, however, is the welfare of first-year students arriving on this campus with a conflicting interest in and revulsion toward "advice" as they leap into this new phase of their education—and of that inevitable handful of continuing students who are returning even though they've never really liked this place all that much.

In spite of my awareness of the repellant nature of anything considered advice, I cannot ignore listing what I've seen in my years on this campus that differentiates those students who survive and thrive from those who are miserable here.

ACTIONS OF TRINITY STUDENTS WHO SURVIVE AND THRIVE:

1. They establish relationships, maintain contact with, and learn to ask for help from faculty advisers, resident mentors, peer tutors, and their class instructors; they get involved in a manageable number of rewarding cocurricular activities.

2. They focus early and diligently on developing time- (and energy-)management skills; they even keep up, fairly well, with all academic tasks/assignments.

3. They eat nutritious meals regularly, get enough sleep to meet their specific needs, avoid abusing alcohol or other drugs, and comply with university conduct policies.

4. They stay in touch with loved ones from home but also establish new friendships with other members of this campus community.

ACTIONS OF TRINITY STUDENTS WHO DO NOT SURVIVE AND THRIVE:

Since I have some rough idea of your SAT scores and high school grades, I know this part will be ever so easy for you. Just reread the above list and revise by inserting "don't" after the word "they" wherever it occurs in each item. (Number 4 requires a tad more polishing; the closing clause needs to begin "nor do they establish.")

As you've surely heard ad nauseam by now, you're a young adult; freedom and independence are yours. You get to choose which list appeals to you. I get to hope.

Life after Graduation

Believe it or not, I've reflected a good bit during our 1979 Spring Break about the mental and emotional state of all my friends who are being graduated this year from dear old TU. Following Spring Break the countdown truly begins, and seniors and master's degree recipients seriously pound the pavement, renew contacts with rich uncles who have "connections" in corporations, and try to discover new and varied routes to the post office so no one will notice how often they check their mail each day for responses from graduate school, Southwestern Bell's training program, or promising school districts.

Mortar Board–Blue Key also reflect on these timely topics and offer a seminar this spring to ponder the provocative question "Is there life after graduation?" I look forward to pondering with them and hearing the wisdom of recent grads.

What does a graduate look for in a job these days?

Geographic location, surely. No one chooses to live in Kansas or Idaho. Appropriate compensation. To avoid humiliation, you've really got to earn as much in your take-home paycheck as your dad's been giving you in allowance these past four years. Aesthetically satisfying environment. This is a hard one, for what home could be prettier than a room on first-floor Winn or third-floor Lightner? Opportunities for advancement. Another serious challenge, for if they want you, the company will hint to the JBF grad that Cronkite retires soon. More likely these days they'll just be vague but upbeat about "limitless possibilities."

I don't do much career counseling, but I've opinions about expectations and priorities in work. The fundamental one is: like what you do or don't do it. Life's far too short to stumble out of bed fifty weeks a year to face unsavory, unethical, or unrewarding chores. Leisure is important, but after college, you'll be appalled at how little of it there really is, and at how little energy and how few resources you possess to enjoy it. Long afternoons previously devoted to viewing the soaps or tossing the Frisbee, pleasant postmidnight snacks at Mi T's, Saturday mornings spent sleeping till noon are very likely soon to be vague memories from your carefree past.

Most of your hours will be devoted to your profession, so please let it be something that excites and stimulates you. If it isn't, settle for less money and more happiness.

Second, I urge upon you an awareness that life's not fair, that you've really not been promised a rose garden. You're not even assured of placement or employment, at the level or location you prefer. And, in spite of all the legislation, you'll find discrimination, injustice, favoritism. Once in a while, you'll see the slackers rewarded and the serious and responsible ridiculed. You can cope with these harsh facts by involving yourself in a long series of lawsuits, or you can heed Voltaire's counsel and "cultivate your own garden." You'd best accept that you can't control anyone else's actions or responses; you'll have enough to do managing your own. All you can do is meet your responsibilities to the best of your ability. You have little control over how your efforts will be perceived, responded to, or rewarded.

So what am I trying to say in all these ramblings? To the graduates, it's rough, but you'll make it, and I think you'll find yourselves uniquely well equipped to adjust to life after graduation and to excel in your chosen field because of your Trinity experience. Most do. To the friends of these graduates I want to say, "Be kind. Be gentle. Be patient. Be understanding." It's a tough but exhilarating stage in the lives of your graduating friends and mine. Treat them well.

Graduation

In a recent interview I said, "I want my students, no matter what their major, to speak well, to write well, to think critically." All that is true, but I didn't have sufficient time to continue my list of wishes for Trinity students, so I'll try to do so subtly in my last short list of this academic year.

It's too late to list exciting opportunities—curricular and cocurricular—available on and off this campus. You've either sampled some of these or you haven't. It's too late to nag about the accessibility of faculty and staff who choose to serve here partly because they welcome the expectation that they advise, guide, and mentor students. You've either developed relationships with some faculty and staff, realizing that this is one of the most valuable aspects offered, or you haven't bothered.

It's even too late to go into my oft-repeated rant that on this campus the only diversity we don't have is intellectual promise, that surrounding you here is a remarkable diversity of economic, geographic, ethnic, spiritual backgrounds. Immersion in such a varied community of intelligent individuals, many of whom are quite different from you, offers exceedingly rare opportunities to stretch, to grow, to evaluate your own views and values. You've either relished that or managed to locate and spend all your time with people who view the world exactly as you do.

What a waste. If you are about to graduate, to transfer, to step out a while, or just to seek a low-paying summer job, and you haven't grasped all that's available to you on this remarkable campus, I, for one, regret your loss.

Bright, articulate, assertive, generally open-minded individuals abound around this place, and, trust me on this one, you will rarely—if ever—enjoy that luxury again in this "best of all possible worlds."

Unless, of course, even if you've not fully benefited from your experiences here, you'll recognize the loss; you'll leave believing that no matter where you go or what you do, you can, sooner or later, try to re-create the climate of support and challenge that you experienced at this institution.

A succinct description of that climate appears in Trinity's Commitment to Excellence, which reads in part, "The university strives to create an atmosphere in which basic civility and decency are respected, mutual respect and open communication are fostered, and sound religious faith and expression are encouraged."

Even if you didn't take advantage of all you might have—of all I wished for you—I'm still hoping you will strive to create such an environment, wherever you go, whatever you do.

I wish you Godspeed.

Getting Ready for the Real World

I've never been a nostalgic person, not for those years of being able to wear size 10 designer dresses and Ferragamo shoes—not even for the few years in which I got a couple of jalapeños on Rate Your Professor. And, although my undergraduate years were mind-opening and provided me with experience in honing my leadership skills as well as my ability to manage time, get sufficient sleep and exercise, and develop lifelong passion for the life of the mind and the rewards of learning, I can't recall nostalgia for the undergraduate years. Perhaps part of the reason is that I never accepted that the college years were the best years of my life. What a depressing cliché! Believe that we peak at about twenty-one or twenty-two, and it's downhill from there? No thank you.

With any luck and some significant effort on our parts when we are undergraduates, the college experience can surely shape our lives, open us to remarkable opportunities, equip us with invaluable skills, and help clarify our values. So I'm sincerely hoping that students soon to graduate, be kicked out, drop out, or transfer will retain some of the best of Trinity's values.

For me, this from the university's Commitment to Excellence conveys those well: "The university strives to create an atmosphere in which basic civility and decency are expected, mutual respect and open communication are fostered, and sound religious faith and expression are encouraged." (Though I did contribute to this document, you can bet those passive verbs weren't mine.)

Surely it's unnecessary to point out that the state of our world has been better—that civil discourse and respect for the opinions, views, and rights of others (especially those in some way different from ourselves) seems on some horrific, seemingly interminable hiatus.

Since you've experienced what I consider much of the best that a liberal arts and sciences education can provide, I sincerely urge you to spread those values and use your talents (to paraphrase Thomas Carlyle) to become all you were created capable of being.

You'll have some challenges. Sadly, you'll rarely—if ever—find yourself surrounded by so many who share your values. In fact, you'll occasionally look around and wonder where in the world all those bright, articulate, and assertive people went. What happened to all those different skin tones, hair, and clothing styles? Some will find appalling the number of white, overweight males who run things wherever you settle. Many of you will surely join a book club and discover that no one but you admires Atwood, McCann, Roth, or Morrison because your new, non-Trinity friends prefer to read books that provide escape rather than challenge them to think. Oh, and, of course, there's got to be a happy ending. (I dare you—and them—to read Atwood's essay by that title.)

But you can make a successful transition—leave "the bubble" and take the best of it with you.

Ever optimistic, I offer these specific suggestions to help ease you into the so-called real world:

1. Avoid jumping to conclusions based on first impressions; give everyone a chance. Be open and accepting, at least until you realize you're being stupid doing so.

2. Without sarcasm or your version of subtle irony, make known your views, even those that differ. Offer some illustrative, supportive detail for your opinions, not all of which need be scriptural.

3. Never, ever use "like" as a filler when you speak.

4. Though you have every reason to do so, do not condescend to those who did not have the privilege of the Trinity experience.

5. Retain (within reason) your sense of self. In a bind—and there will be binds—recite silently the Red Queen's advice to Alice: "Use French when you don't know the English word for a thing, walk with your toes out, and remember who you are."

I sincerely believe you can manage to be "all that you were created capable of being" and that doing so will include conducting yourself as a person who contributes to making this a better world—a world more guided by a "commitment to excellence."

I will miss many of you, and I sincerely wish you all Godspeed.

Hope Chest

At the March 27, 2003, Service Awards Ceremony,
President John Brazil presented me with a mantel clock
(maroon/white with gold Trinity seal and trim) commem-
orating my forty years of service to this institution. (Never
mind that I have really worked here forty-three and a half
years; I did resign once upon a time in 1961 because trying
to enforce 8:30 p.m. curfews for women residing in Myrtle,
Isabel, and Susanna was putting me over the edge, and I
decided to forgo student personnel work and earn a Ph.D.
in English so I might have an easier life. Silly me.)

Called "girls" in those days, these Trinity undergraduates were about as easy to intimidate as our students are
today; imagine the speed with which these young adults
checked in at 8:25 p.m. and then departed via their private balconies by 8:45 p.m. Devoting my energies to cor-
ralling them was not within my capabilities, and I simply
couldn't stand that the men had no rules while women
had everything from absurd curfews to "appropriate dress
standards."

What did appeal a couple of years later was a
$6,000 annual salary offer from President Laurie to

return to student personnel and, over time, perhaps help bring about some changes in the quality of Trinity student life.

With all those Trinity years to guide me, I leapt at the opportunity to offer some of my hopes for those in the Class of 2003 as they prepare to be graduated and to become lifetime members of the Trinity University Alumni Association:

1. As you endeavor to create a safe haven—or even a cocoon—for yourself and those you love, I hope you will appreciate the irony if that haven sometimes resembles a bubble.

2. One of these days, I hope you'll realize that although this university has never yet enrolled as many ethnic minorities as we would like, ethnicity is not the only diversity; in this community I trust that you came to know, to admire, to respect, and, even to love, many persons very different from yourself.

3. As a graduate of a liberal arts and sciences institution, I hope that in your wide-ranging interests you will reflect upon the rewards of such a liberating education.

4. I hope that "simplicity, lucidity, and euphony" characterize everything you write, and that you'll always try "to say what you mean and to mean what you say."

5. Though you've surely heard this enough by now, try to cope with the fact that the sacrifices of your family and the generosity of donors to this institution enabled you to have the enriching experience of a Trinity education. I hope you'll offer your support to others as these have to you.

6. The two regrets of my life are that I didn't have a dog of my own until I was thirty-five or a cat until I was fifty-two. Don't waste time. As Maxine Kumin puts it, "How we treat the animals in our keeping defines us as human beings." Be well defined as soon as possible.

7. Learn to value your own company. Consider D. H. Lawrence's words: "To be alone is one of life's greatest delights, thinking one's own thoughts, doing one's own little jobs, seeing the world beyond and feeling oneself uninterrupted in the rooted connection with the center of all things."

8. I hope, sooner rather than later, as the cliché goes, you will learn to appreciate the absurd, to laugh at yourself. Please cultivate a sense of humor to help you deal with whatever life throws your way.

9. Katharine Graham wrote, "To love what you do and feel that it matters. How could anything be more fun?" I hope that you will find, as I have found, such work—make it matter, make it fun.

10. Finally, I hope, as a Trinity University graduate, you'll regularly recite to yourself the Red Queen's words to Alive and that you'll follow that advice: "Use French when you don't know the English word for a thing, walk with your toes out and remember who you are."

I know you will make us proud, and I wish you Godspeed.

Alumni

Alumni Come Home

Students now, in 1978, are bound to wonder what it will be like when they are Trinity graduates, November rolls around, and it is Homecoming time. While you're here the time is simply filled with significant traumas such as whether or not you'll have a date for the dance; you'll find your way to the sorority off-campus parties; your club's booth will collapse at Fiesta; your roommate's out-of-town boyfriend, here for the weekend, will ever return to his home.

But when you've left and are out coping with life after graduation, you'll think of old TU and have different worries: Will they take your diploma away if you don't contribute to the Alumni Fund? Will someone figure out you never really understood calculus or *Paradise Lost* and send a refund on your tuition money for your sophomore year? Is the campus still beautifully landscaped, well-tended, and swarming with friendly, occasionally grubby young people? Are there still instructors who observe office hours, go to coffee with you, or even to the Bombay? Do people still learn and grow and care about each other even while they make jokes about the "country club of the Southwest" and "the university in the sun"?

I can't answer the current queries for you, except to assure you that few Fiesta booths fall. Some should, god knows, but few do. But I can address these for the alums: Diplomas aren't refunded, nor is tuition money. Though much has changed, all that is essential about this unique campus remains the same. There's still tons of apathy— can apathy come in tons? Many students still rarely have dates even to highlighted seasonal events. Caring, committed faculty and staff almost inundate this place. Fiscal resources are still handled wisely with remarkable insight and foresight. The campus is cared for, the curriculum is reviewed, and the faculty is encouraged, both philosophically and financially, to develop themselves. Standards for admission rise. A new library fulfills a dream. Inspiring, dynamic leadership hovers on the horizon with the arrival of Ron Calgaard as our new president.

You mutter, "She's prejudiced." You recall that at the annual musical competition, Sing Song, we always heard the joke about my coming to Trinity in a covered wagon. (Never mind the tasteless punch line, "When you see her up close you'll understand why the wagon was covered!") If I'm prejudiced about this place, I have good reason to be. I've watched it grow; I've consulted with colleagues and students from other schools; I've made comparisons.

The trivial irritations and disappointments are much clearer while you're here, of course; I can't convince you. But just wait. When you are gone, you'll be proud that this is the alma mater you come home to.

Alumni Weekend and All Its "Pleasures"

The alums are coming! The alums are coming! Trinity's Alumni Weekend looms on the horizon with its influx of current and potential donors and supporters of their beloved alma mater. Some surely look back on their years on this halcyon campus as the "happiest years of their lives," as parents and high school teachers so often assure youngsters these years will be—hoping that no one will bother to wonder what this might bode for all the decades following college. Others, alas, hold grudges about their undergraduate experience. It's those I am far from eager to see.

Except for the last nine years of my career, I wasn't "only an English teacher." For the four preceding decades I'd held titles ranging from head resident to associate dean of student life to dean of students and vice president for student affairs. I was, you see, one of those charged with enforcing rules of conduct and acting among the first responders in crises.

Most of those reading this (if anyone, in fact, is) are current students fully aware of and grateful for the enlightened policies—the respect for rights of individuals, including students; the delicious, varied, and reasonably priced food plans; the well-maintained and competently managed residence halls; the focused, inspiring, accessible faculty. I could go on and on, but you get the idea. You know who and where you are and cannot even imagine having anything about which to hold a grudge against Trinity.

These are no doubt young adults who already understand the wisdom of these lines from novelist John P. Marquand: "Perhaps the best way of judging whether or not certain years in your life were happy might be to determine how much you remembered about them; for the happiest years were those in which events blended with each other so naturally that all that remained was a recollection of growth and achievement."

That's what I would wish the recollections of graduates of Trinity University to be. So the question is, why would I, with my many years of service on this campus, feel even a twinge of dread with hundreds of alums invading campus for a weekend?

Let me answer this by listing just a sampling of the questions I usually get at these gatherings: What's the curfew for the girls' dorms? (As if a dorm and not the girls would have a curfew . . . but I digress.) Why are *you* wearing slacks on upper campus? What happened to the dress code? Have you gotten rid of those "Greeks" yet? Why wasn't my son admitted here? Is it true that you let boys and girls reside in the same dorms?

What's this honor code thing? What do you mean students receive due process? Why would you permit that? Why did you quit giving tennis scholarships? How old is Leroy now?

What happened to the Crystal Pistol? Is there still a Bombay Bicycle Club? Do you enforce the twenty-one-year-old drinking age? Do you miss the days when the legal age was eighteen? Why's the library so big? Who moved the Eugenia Miller Fountain?—I could swear it was on the other side of Northrup. Whose cats are those?

Now do you have a smattering of an idea of the reasons for my anxiety (or is "dread" too strong a word?) about Alumni Weekend? If you don't yet, consider this: inevitably many alums will greet me with this assertion, which I try to believe is well-intended: "Dean/Dr. Grissom! You haven't changed a bit."

What do you think this says about what I must have looked like when I was thirty? forty? fifty? sixty? Or even seventy?

I am one who is quick to see the glass half full, so I comfort myself by realizing that I would be far more depressed if the alums greeted me with "Good gracious, how did you get so old? Didn't you use to be a perfect size 10? What happened to your neck? Are those gnarled fingers I see?"

In case anyone does say anything like that to me—in case I have to respond to such candor, I am practicing saying, "This is simply a result of having my life touched over five decades by bright, self-assured little weasels such as you. I am just keeping on, keeping on. Get over it."

Wish me luck!

Avoiding Nostalgia

In spite of my advanced age, I am not now nor have I ever been a nostalgic person. Even as I was experiencing my childhood, youth, and middle age, I don't think I ever thought, "These are the good old days—I'll miss them sometime."

For some unknown bizarre reason, I've always been an in-the-moment person; this may well change as decrepitude creeps up on me (does it creep or just arrive suddenly, by surprise?) with losses of mental and physical capacities, but if so, that will be yet another adjustment, one in attitude as well as abilities. Maybe this will be the trigger to creating nostalgia in me.

How could I be nostalgic? What would I be nostalgic for? The deprivations of growing up in the Great Depression or the years of World War II with its rationing, Victory Gardens, and the threat of invading Nazi storm troopers or Japanese in their submarines sneaking up on us in East Texas?

Should I be nostalgic for those sexist-driven years of high school, graduate school, and early career—years in which a "woman's place was in the home," and, if she did happen to stumble into any conference rooms, she was the one expected to serve the coffee, and if she ran for an office in an organization, that office would have to be secretary? I'm not feeling nostalgic yet, are you?

For most decades of my life, expectations of decorous conduct and attire ruled for women and for women only—no shorts on upper campus, gloves, hat, heels, hose (with straight seams always) when leaving campus, hair back-combed in a bouffant and tightly sprayed. Obviously, I don't mourn the passing of those days, as my hairstyle and wardrobe for the last several decades loudly proclaim.

My avoidance of nostalgia could be changing. After being a member of the Trinity community for more than fifty years, I must admit that following our annual Alumni Weekend, I do briefly experience something that resembles a slight wish to return to a former time until I examine that feeling more closely.

Perhaps I should have expected this because of the weird fact (yes, even to me) that I am still teaching when many of my former students are gleefully relishing retirement.

Although I know that I am not doing this to support a drug or gambling addiction, I sometimes think that might be easier to explain than the simple truth: I continue to do what I love and to love what I do. (Katharine Graham put it this way: "To love what you do and feel that it matters—how could anything be more fun?") I still find teaching Trinity students challenging, demanding, exhausting, sometimes frustrating, but almost always fun. And, because of the quality of these young adults, I feel that what I do does matter. With each passing year, perhaps the reason I don't become nostalgic is that I am still doing what brings me the most joy.

Visiting with alums when they're on campus focuses my attention on the blessings I have so long enjoyed in this community and explains what should be obvious: I don't miss this because I still have it.

Spending some time with those who've shared the "Trinity experience" reminds me of certain verities. For example, some aspects of the diversity of the returning graduates were astonishing: lawyers, doctors, teachers, administrators, coaches, "stay-at-home moms," accountants, social service workers, missionaries, artists, ministers, writers, and on and on. Widows, defeated political candidates, recently elected political candidates, divorcees; an almost unseemly few still happily married to the person they met during New Student Orientation; there were gays with partners, gays without partners, and even an alum I knew as a young woman who is now a handsome young man.

These Trinity graduates came from all over the world to celebrate their years here and renew acquaintances, and, as usual, even though I was immediately aware of their diversity, it was easy to realize that the common denominators remained the same as always—they all possessed a healthy sense of self and were both intelligent and articulate. This didn't make me nostalgic, since I still deal with such young adults daily, but it did emphasize some of the lasting characteristics resulting from "the Trinity experience."

Many alums sent emails after they returned home, and these convey the spirit and the qualities that abide: "reflection as to where I have been and where I am going." "No matter what time has done to us, we can sit down together and immediately recognize what it was we liked about each other fifty years ago." "Having lifelong friends who are interesting, intelligent, caring, and downright fun is valuable beyond words." "Looking around at my class-mates at Flats, I choked up and realized 'these people saved my life once. . . . I can't imagine how I would have made it through that year without the Trinity community. What a gift.'"

Several addressed what-ifs—what if they had gone to SMU, Baylor, Duke, Tech, or UT, as they'd first consid-ered—and everyone commented on their gratitude for Trinity's philosophy, curriculum, accessible faculty com-mitted to teaching undergraduates, and their "amazing" peers, many of whom "are still tightly woven" into their lives.

Considering these enduring reflections on their time here, it came as no surprise to me that my current stu-dents' lists of what they like least about Trinity closely par-alleled what also made the alums cranky when they were here—really obnoxious challenges, such as Cardiac Hill, enormous tuition, limited food choices, difficult classes, and being unable to hide. (Current students also included "the construction," but some alums even had to survive the building of 281, on which several now gratefully commute.)

The recurrent recollections most valued are the quality of education in and out of the classroom and the "bonding experience of living in the dorm," where lifelong friendships formed. Although what made these relationships last cannot be quantified, the Trinity experience, which includes the quality of individuals sharing it and the learning environment created, surely plays a critical role.

I have always cherished a line from the university's Commitment to Excellence document and quote it every chance I get: "The university strives to create an atmosphere in which basic civility and decency are expected, mutual respect and open communication are fostered, and sound religious faith and expression are encouraged."

Though the reliance on passive-voice verbs in the statement makes my teeth hurt, I cherish the blessing of being able to spend my career in a university community based on such a foundation. Only when I no longer have this blessing will I be nostalgic.

Alums

A couple of weekends ago was Trinity University's Alumni Weekend, 2000, which brings to campus hundreds of graduates, some of whom live nearby and frequently attend events on campus; others reside in every place imaginable (some even unimaginable) and haven't been on campus in decades but come back for significant reunion years.

Following my Saturday morning speech, "Down Memory Lane and Beyond," Selim Sharif, associate director of alumni relations, led me to room 357 in the Dicke/Smith building, where I was to meet with members of the Class of '63.

Gracious as always, Selim pretended to ignore that I'd snatched two chocolate chip cookies and a cup containing the dregs of the lukewarm coffee off the hospitality table, and, once in the room, he busied himself doing what exemplary staff persons do—he arranged the desks in a large circle in order to create an environment that he knew I wanted, one that would encourage informal conversation.

Somewhat apprehensively, I began by asking these alums to take a few minutes to tell us some highlights of the past fifty years. (I didn't dare ask, "So what have you been up to this last half century?" Doing so, however, did cross my mind.)

In hindsight, it wasn't surprising that they were all articulate and vulnerable; not a single one used "like" or "basically" as a filler. They did, however, speak from their hearts.

As is so often the case with Trinity people—whether long-ago graduates or contemporary ones—these individuals took my inane request and ran with it, succinctly telling us where they'd lived, what other education they'd had, what professions they'd followed, what hobbies fascinated them. They spoke openly of losses—spouses, children—and several of the men commented on their service in the military, mostly in Vietnam; following my inevitable mention of pets, a few of the more nervy ones even tried to outdo me with obviously hyperbolic comments about theirs.

The tone of our conversation wasn't nostalgic, as I'd expected it might be, but when they spoke of their years at and memories of Trinity, they—to a person—commented on the marvelous, accessible, supportive faculty, their remarkable peers (several of whom had married one another), and the challenges and learning gained from the Trinity residential life experience.

Admittedly, one man asked me to absolve him for getting lost on the way back to the dorms, making his date late for her curfew. She was at the meeting with her husband; this bad-influence date, with his wife. Apparently, I had mandated a three-weekend campus penalty on the woman, even though he was responsible for her lateness by getting lost.

He wanted forgiveness, which, Lord knows, I was happy to give, though I couldn't help but hope he hadn't been brooding over this for all these years. (Rules are rules, you know, and, in those "good old days," only women had any.)

I finally introduced nostalgia by mentioning my appreciation of Earl Abel's restaurant, long located at Hildebrand and Broadway, but now farther out on Austin Highway. I reminded the group that this was the only restaurant in the city that would let me and some of the women students enter when accompanied by our one black student, whose name, I, of course, and everyone in the room, recalled.

After my recollection, one of the alums shared an even more moving one: she, a couple of friends, and this same lone black student joined a sit-in at the Woolworth counter downtown. As they tried to eat their bowls of chili, they were harassed, their heads shoved into their bowls, and subjected to the usual epithets of that ugly era.

Being Trinity students, they reacted angrily, defending themselves, but they soon learned that they had "flunked" the training for sit-ins because they had failed to comply with Dr. King's insistence that they not respond in kind, no matter how cruel the mistreatment, how harsh the words.

We all shared their shame in being kicked out of sit-in training, but once again, all of us felt immense pride when reminded of the quality of human beings who have built this institution.

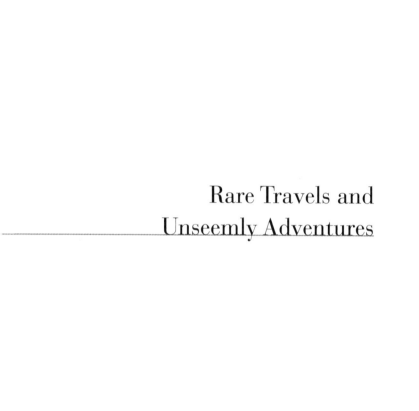

Rare Travels and
Unseemly Adventures

Colorado Rockies

"How was your summer, Dean Grissom?" they ask. Busy, hot, exhausting, rejuvenating, rewarding—never boring. Two weekends spent in June at our Parents' Orientation started the summer months with the refreshing company of the concerned parents of new students as they sought so eagerly to better equip themselves to assist their children during their undergraduate experience.

Writing those challenging form letters to new and returning students occupied much time early in the summer as I tried to convey such information as the date the dormitories open for the fall with a fresh and interesting style! Holding the attention of an undergraduate student through the reading of an entire page of written material in the summer (or at any other time, for that matter) isn't easy.

Mid-July brought the start of three glorious weeks in Colorado, highlighted by an experience perhaps best described as "interesting" when I went, ignorant of social norms, to the Paradise Hot Tub Spa.

Absentminded and spacey as I tend to be late in the day, I was nevertheless quick to notice that no one in the tub except myself and my friend was wearing a stitch of clothing. Swimming trunks were seemingly out of style in Crested Butte. Tastefully attired in my bright purple Catalina, I splashed the water around me as vigorously as I dared and conversed in a somewhat squeaky octave with the young men and women lolling in the water around me. I couldn't help but notice that they stared at my suit disapprovingly, and I, for once, felt ashamed of it, too.

The only blessing of this adventure was that one bather remarked that I'd enjoy the spa more after 5 p.m. when the city's construction crew arrived. As you might guess, a middle-aged woman reared in East Texas has the sense to leave before 5 p.m. And so I did.

The rest of the vacation was less eventful: long hikes on high mountain trails, collapsing under trees to remove the backpack, snarf gorp (trail mix, for you non-hikers), and swill lukewarm canteen water, photographing Colorado's Coors-producing streams and waterfalls, gripping the seat as the jeep tour driver forged new paths across meadows and up precipices obviously never traversed except by goats, picnicking in the safety of the car in a heavy hailstorm high atop Cumberland Pass (12,000 feet, billed as the highest standard car pass in the United States), improving my musical taste by listening to the Top 40 on my portable radio in front of a roaring late-July fire, and reading mostly trash except for one provocative novel about a presence too often in my life, the "Under Toad."

Home in early August I felt relaxed and almost laid back, but I was immediately hit by the blast of energy coming out of the office of the president of Trinity University. Suddenly I found myself caught up in lengthy meetings, sitting at my desk until late in the evening, going home for a quick supper and spending the rest of the night thrilling my poodles by speaking in my dulcet tones into my portable Dictaphone. And, will you believe it? Loving almost every minute of it.

In case you've missed it, there is exhilaration spreading through this campus, an excitement, a dynamic force, a new sense of commitment, of order, of attention to detail.

Take my word for it, we're entering an eventful and momentous era for this institution. It may not be as interesting as the Paradise Hot Tub Spa, but I wouldn't take any bets if I were you.

Fear of Flying

I don't fly very often, but this past Saturday I flew to Dallas and back to speak at another Admissions Office seminar for prospective students. Not exactly elated to hear my alarm go off, I nevertheless respected my commitment, stumbled out of bed, walked my dogs, breakfasted, and prepared to catch the 9 a.m. flight.

My friend John Moore, wandering the terminal looking for trouble as is his wont, happened by the door as I entered, so guided me through what are to this inexperienced flier the intricacies of boarding the right flight.

Entering the rather surprisingly small plane, at first I thought it was 1953 again and I was stepping onto another Greyhound for the trek from Commerce to Carthage. The stylishness of persons who fly seems to have deteriorated in the past several years.

Fashion conscious as always, I blinked twice as I saw that the stewards were wearing orange hot pants. Was this what's called jet lag? I couldn't help myself as I marveled at the anachronism of hot pants in 1979—and in 32-degree weather!

I observed Trinity faculty, staff, and students on the plane and counted their white knuckles reassuringly. Deans Boyd and Kramer sat with Chairperson Symons, and all appeared to be solving a few problems of the world—or at least of the university—as they chatted. Boyd made a lot of notes on a large yellow pad, Kramer sometimes let his eyes (and, I suspect, his mind) wander out the window, and Symons occasionally thumbed an issue of *Harper's* (no doubt inspired to find the Sawhill article, "The Unlettered University" [February 1979], that I mentioned in my recent essay).

Since we weren't flying first class, I was delighted to be served free coffee, but my delight was short-lived when I became suspicious of my Styrofoam cup. It had a tiny chunk torn out of the lip which I felt sure some other white-knuckled passenger had bitten out on a previous flight when the plane went through an air pocket.

John and I talked Trinity a little, dogs a lot, and plans for the rest of the weekend until I noticed that the chapter title in a book the lady on the other side of me was reading was "Mashed Potato Love." Soon I tuned John out and tried to scan over her shoulder surreptitiously, to no avail. When we arrived in Dallas, the differentiation between duties of deans and chairpersons was made painfully obvious: Business's George Thompson efficiently corralled four cabs to take us from the airport to the Hilton, Chairpersons Murray and Howland lugged audiovisual equipment, and, when we got to the hotel, the deans placed the coffee orders.

The seminar itself at the Hilton was classy in the usual Trinity way. Obviously affluent parents of current students mingled with alums looking for work. (Well, to be perfectly honest, only one was unemployed: most of the alums were in high-ranking professional roles.) I wandered down memory lane with wonderful men and women I hadn't seen in years, devoured a delicious meal, delivered a satisfactorily well-received speech, and cabbed it back to Love Field and the hot pants set. Waiting to board the homeward flight, I tried not to overhear an irate elderly lady shriek to the boarding pass distributor, "Your airline burned out my hearing aid batteries. I have to go to a party tonight. I can't hear. And you're sorry?" I did feel compassion for her problem, but mostly I yearned to help her improve her sentence variety.

On the plane I scanned May Sarton's *Journal of a Solitude* and pondered this thoughtful paragraph: "Does anything in nature not seem to despair. It is too busy trying to survive. It is all closed in to a kind of still, intense waiting. Is this a key? Keep busy with survival. Imitate the trees. Learn to lose in order to recover, and remember that nothings stays the same for long, not even pain, psychic pain. Sit it out. Let it all pass. Let it go."

The plane wasn't so crowded on the way home, but a strange aroma invaded my sensitive nostrils. Some odor from my childhood in East Texas. What was that smell?

Finally, I realized the plane contained several booted fellows headed for the rodeo in San Antonio. That was the memorable aroma of manure I was recalling.

John Moore had queried on the way up, "Who do you think will get the headlines if the plane goes down?" And when it didn't, he had observed, as I was taking an earlier flight home, "If that one goes, Coleen, you get all the headlines." A most reassuring observation to a woman who lives by this cliché: "If she had wanted us to fly, she'd have given us wings."

But I did get home and have been given more time not only to despair now and again, but also to ponder such significances as what to do about student storage, how high to build a fence, how to get students to bother to carry keys if we install better locks, to keg or not to keg, and what essay topics will really shake up the little punks on the midsemester?

It's good to be on solid ground again. Thank you, God.

Trip to the Spa

Fortifying myself in what I deemed an appropriate fashion for my initial visit to Trim & Swim Health spa, I dined on spaghetti Thursday night and devoured slabs of barbecued beef on Friday. "Keep your strength up," obese relatives ever advised me as a child.

Fully cognizant of my well-nourished strength, I stuffed myself into what I have labeled my "in no way saggy" black leotards and motored to Trim & Swim. The cars in the parking lot were my first hint of trouble; they all seemed big for the road, and some appeared to have overinflated tires. Dismissing these observations as typical Grissom superstition, I presented myself to Betsy for the ordeal of weigh-in, measuring, and preparation of goal chart.

Blessedly, I was privileged to wait in line before these moments of truth behind a needier case: a five-foot two-inch, 195-pound, postmenopausal matron whose thigh appeared about the size of my waist when encased in my best girdle. Realizing the matron was most likely a plant stationed there just to give hope to the lost who might still have time to stop payment on enrollment checks,

I nevertheless faced bravely these requirements. I squinted like Lily Tomlin (when she's doing Ernestine or watching John Travolta drop his towel). I didn't want to do a Tomlin impersonation, but I did want to close my eyes as best I could, for the measuring cruelly takes place in a mirror-lined room. Betsy proved herself well trained, for she never once cracked a smile, much less chortled aloud as I had anticipated.

Betsy led me around the exercise room "introducing" me to a variety of machines, the use of which could perform, in time, small miracles. There is no question in my mind but that each of these is a modernized version of a relic found in the dungeons of such castles as I was familiar with from my reading of *The Mysteries of Udolpho*. One was recognizable from my visit to the hamster section of pet stores, so, puffing out my cheeks, I, too, climbed upon a treadmill.

I treaded eventually off the treadmill and eased my way by creeping along supporting myself on the wall into the "wet area." Misunderstanding why all the ladies were avoiding the first shower on the left, I stepped in, pulled the chain, and was doused with the world's coldest downpour of ice water. I shrieked at a decibel and at a pitch I never knew myself capable of while all the waiting ladies giggled appreciatively.

Moving more rapidly, I realized I was, in spite of myself, becoming a convert to the spa. I collapsed in the wonderfully relaxing sauna, steam room, and whirlpool, and I splashed in the cool swimming pool; after a moment in each of these I began to experience the exhilaration of self-pride that comes from physical exertion and discipline of self.

As I dressed in the narrow aisle, I locked eyes proudly with women who, like myself, looked younger, more self-assured, and far fitter than they had an hour ago. With a firmly set jaw and quivering biceps, I accelerated past Mr. Gatti's on my way home.

Fetishes and Compulsions

Dieting

Sunday, March 18. For the first time in my forty-five and a half years, I am seriously observing a diet. Labeled as the U.S. Ski Team's Diet, the verbiage promised, "You may lose as much as twenty pounds in two weeks." I'm allowed to eat many tasty treats, highlighted by rubbery hard-boiled eggs and tart grapefruit.

***

Monday, March 19. I am suffering psychologically and physiologically and have new respect for all my friends who diet regularly. I'm convinced that one has not truly suffered until one has experienced carbohydrate withdrawal. Psychologically, I became snappish at one end of the scale today and weepy at the other. Early in the day, when a friend, observing my culinary efforts, remarked, "That's not the way you make iced tea," I didn't respond with an explanation of my chosen process. I simply threw the boiling water into the sink, stomped from the room, and shrieked back over my shoulder, "I don't have to defend myself to you." Whatever that meant, I'll never know.

***

Tuesday, March 20. Things grow worse. When my secretary told me this morning, "You've a couple of calls to return," I whimpered, brushed back tears, and asked her to dial for me, just this once. Nothing interests me. Without food I'm not attentive to conversation, music, or the needs of others.

Without food I've developed a new skill for me: I have learned to procrastinate.

***

Wednesday, March 21. The Sing Song script lies untouched on my desk; just think, I may end up having to repeat old jokes! What will the students think? Physiologically, I am a wreck. I've probably had fewer than twenty headaches in twenty years. Suddenly I've had two in two days. I still have my appendix and enjoy a pretty sturdy digestive tract, so excruciating stomach cramps during the last three days have been an innovation I happily could have done without. (In classes yesterday, I resorted to sitting on the table so I could gracefully rest my arms on my stomach and relieve pains by quick, and, I hope, unnoticeable pressure from my elbows.)

***

Thursday, March 22. In this foray into the world of the dieter I have relearned much that I had forgotten about the psychological effects of physiological deprivation. I had foolishly thought that while I was spending less time eating I would have more time to appreciate friends, read, listen to music.

Instead, in my newfound leisure, I have become obsessed with food. In an appointment today my eyes wandered to the chubby calves of one of my visitors, and I daydreamed of leg of lamb as she spoke and the recipes in Swift's "A Modest Proposal." After supper tonight (I had a poached egg and half a leaf of spinach), instead of appreciating Beethoven's Symphony No. 6, the "Pastoral," more than ever, I found myself trying to chew the knobs off the stereo. My other senses have not compensated at all; they did not become more acute. They were dulled and suddenly insensitive. I realized that without food I was worse than a carnivore; I'm an extremely hungry, quite pitiful carnivore.

***

Friday, March 23. I'm feeling remarkably rejuvenated today and have continued to supplement my diet with some of my favorite quick energy preferences, have felt as perky as a sorority pledge, and have managed to lose three to four pounds during the week. I've reconciled myself to the fact that I'll never look like a member of the U.S. Ski Team, but I've also realized that I probably don't need to in sunny San Antonio so far from the slopes.

Collecting Moments

"People forget years and remember moments"—so asserts one of my favorite short story writers, Ann Beattie. Believing her words, I've been recollecting moments that define the summer of 2013, and part of what I realize is that I not only recall moments but also recall, almost as clearly, the moment after the moment. After thoughtful analysis, I've concluded that what I thought was the memorable moment was just the preamble to its antithesis, which often occurs immediately afterward.

This summer, being the good little (albeit anxious and neurotic) trooper that I am, I dragged myself out of bed one morning before 5 a.m., shoving snoring poodles out of the way so that I could, with a friend serving as chauffeur, find my way in the predawn light to the Gastroenterology Clinic of San Antonio on scenic Datapoint Drive. Having survived the demeaning delights of the colonoscopy and marveling once again that Katie Couric once had hers performed on live television, I obligingly kept my follow-up appointment at the physician's office the next week.

I thought my memorable moment was that relieving one when Dr. Jorge Muñoz stated, "No polyps, nothing of concern. All clear." But it was his next observation that most struck me: "Unless some problem develops, you shouldn't need ever to have this procedure again."

Why did I so quickly switch my recollected moment? Well, just think about it for a minute. What the doctor was saying in a discreet way was something like, "You'll be too old to bother." Or, worse yet, "You'll probably be long gone." Although this realization didn't make me regret that I got an "all clear" result, it certainly caught my attention and embedded in my memory the bad news that so often quickly follows the good. Who knew it would ever give me pause to have a gastroenterologist tell me that I wouldn't need another colonoscopy?

Another late summer moment I thought would be a long-recollected happy highlight was the humane trapping of two young feral cats and securing them on my screened back porch after having them immunized and neutered. My friends and I had saved them from a danger-filled life, assured that they were healthy, prevented their breeding more feral cats, and provided a safe, comfortable home.

That should have been the moment to remember, but alas, they remained wild as March hares—however wild that might be. They would not get near me, prevented my indoor cats and dogs from having any access to their beloved porch, and mastered a look of terror, with pupils so dilated the kittens appeared to be trapped in a refilming of *Invasion of the Body Snatchers*.

As the hated cliché goes, "to make a short story long," I must reveal that the moment we trapped the cats a second time—this time *on* my porch—and safely released them in the grove of trees from which they'd come was the memorable moment, the diametrical opposite of what I first thought.

Already this fall I've relished many lovely moments which I hope to remember, most of which have to do with returning to the classroom after my academic leave this spring and the long, hot, dry summer in the boonies. But again, I have to concentrate on not focusing prematurely on what I'll recollect.

Hard as it is for some to believe, teachers are nervous on the first days of classes, and I struggle not to overreact to the blank, bored, unengaged faces of the young adults before me—their fingers practically twitching to reach their cell phones and their look of dismay when I announce that I accept only essays printed on something called paper. They hate me. That's my first moment that imprinted on my mind.

The admissions staff's proud announcement of increased diversity sits there as fifteen individuals before me. I struggle to pronounce names, wondering where all the Joneses, Smiths, and Johnsons have gone, and, nervous about this, I immediately insist on addressing a woman to my right as Rachel, and one across from me as Hannah, when everyone but me realizes the names are just the opposite. They, especially Hannah and Rachel, hate me.

Thankfully, I've now taught five days of classes, and it's as if enrollment has totally changed: bright, prepared, engaged, articulate young adults have somehow replaced those of that first class session! Most of the time I address them by their correct name and don't mangle the pronunciation too badly. Maybe they don't hate me. Maybe they just think I'm not as tech-friendly or cosmopolitan as they. Maybe they think we will grow and learn together.

You see, as long as I don't—another hideous cliché that makes absolutely no sense—"jump the gun," I have positive, enriching, reassuring moments to collect and to cherish. At the top of my short list this week is making certain I choose my moments well and urging you to do the same.

Keeping a Daily Journal

Decades ago when I occasionally had the question-able privilege of putting my young nieces and nephew—Kathy, Krista, and Kerry—to bed, after their prayers, I started asking them, in hopes of encouraging both a sense of gratitude and pleasant dreams, "What was your happi-est time today?"

Generally, this worked well and sometimes I could react to the chosen response or experiences without being sanctimonious or moralistic. I do recall a few slipups. When having been mean to a sibling or gotten away with some indiscretion made the happy times list, I couldn't resist pointing out that certain behaviors really shouldn't make anyone's happiest times list. But I digress.

Along the way, when, for reasons not recollected, I started keeping a journal, writing in it just before bedtime each evening, I closed each entry of that day's activities with my own short notations of happiest times. Doing this then and now fully focuses me on gratitude for my many blessings and surprisingly underscores how mundane and ordinary the highlights of most of my days are. Having been officially recognized for some achievement seems rarely to make the list, but taking a hot bath or having written a caring note to a friend frequently does.

This aspect of my journal keeping surely played a considerable role in my celebrating the mundane and recognizing the importance of valuing it. I've even collected several lines from writers I admire in which they seem to celebrate this also.

Not surprisingly, John Updike expresses it best: "My only duty was to describe reality as it had come to me—to give the mundane its beautiful due."

But I think I admire this from the film writer Frank Perry almost as much: "Nothing is more important than the holiness of everyday life. The sanctity of the ordinary, the mundane, the minutia of life. To lose sight of it is tragic."

Scribbling the happiest times of my day in a journal concentrates my attention on this sanctity and the ordinariness of what fulfills me.

The presence of several boxes full of journals provides me with my own private and personal reference library. Annually, I scan through that year's journal and compile my lists of books I've read that I want to recommend to others in my end-of-the-year newsletter; also, of course, by flipping through the twelve months of daily entries, I can recall highlights and low points of the year, television I admired, experiences and rare travels that are worth sharing with others. And, unfortunately, the journals also bring to light the issues, political and personal, which distressed me—everything from deaths of loved ones to the ongoing triumphs of right-wing conspirators to the destruction of our beautiful planet by, among others, the "climate change deniers." I rant to my journals, so closing with happiest times becomes critical to peace of mind, but also, surely, venting my spleen privately is healthy as well.

Ranting to my journals has, I believe, been a release and beats ranting on a street corner or in an administrative office. Long before I felt it was an injustice and even longer before I realized it was illegal, I confided to my journal the slights and discrimination I felt in my work based on my gender: a significantly lower salary than male colleagues at the same rank, no vice president title although I carried the same level of responsibility, no university car assigned to me—and, before that, of course, no car telephone, no invitation to many of the "top-level" meetings even though student affairs concerns were often involved, and, until the board of trustees awarded me the vice president title, no university residence.

I whined about these matters to my journal but otherwise tried to keep silent. I blamed the oversights to my being less valued because the chief executive and trustees found my work less effective than that of my peers, but even as I belittled my skills and contributions, I felt I was insincere. I believed I was at least as capable as most and, honestly, better than some.

Only once did I ask for a raise. President James W. Laurie, whom I adored and esteemed, simply replied to me with an unanswerable question: "What does a sweet young thing like you need with money? You'll get married someday, and your husband will take good care of you." I still wonder how that wise, good man could have been so wrong about my future.

Friends who knew me well were cognizant of my discomfort with the many formal social requirements of my administrative role, but my journal entries contained more details than persons. My distaste for small talk itself and the subjects of most small talk at such events—prowess at hunting, brilliance of Republican leadership, homophobia, racism, acquisitiveness—appalled, distressed, and saddened me. I learned the truth of the adage "I drink to make other people more interesting." (I would add "and more bearable.")

My journal has also long served as the outlet for some of my terrors: disease; loss; anonymous, threatening, wee-hour telephone calls; stalking by a disturbed student; learning that angry fraternity members had erected a replica of an execution structure and tiny cloth poodles hanging from nooses. Retiring from my administrative role certainly relieved me of many of those distresses.

Historically, my journals depress me because, along with various unpleasant reminders of regrettable choices, they underscore frustrations, slights, heartbreaks of both my personal and professional life. I rarely reread them because of this and because of my deteriorating script. Sometimes, however, I look up what I scribbled on what I considered a particularly significant day, such as on

March 2, 1968, when I commented on a newspaper article concerning a student tossing a soda bottle at LBJ during an appearance at the University of Texas in Austin. The head of the board of regents said, "When we've gotten to the point where we need 300 armed policemen to guard the president on a visit to a college campus, we need to look again at what higher education is all about."

I was attending a student personnel administrators' conference in Chicago in 1968 at the same time as the Democratic Convention and received rare long-distance calls from my East Texas family urging me to stay in the hotel. Martin Luther King Jr. had been assassinated on April 4, and the next evening I wrote, "I am frightened by the news of the National Guardsmen being called out because of fires and looting. Four so far have been killed. How sad that the death of a man who tried to teach nonviolence should result in an excuse for young punks to set fires, burn, and, most especially, loot."

When the seemingly endless assassinations continued, I didn't know of Robert Kennedy's until I noticed "sad faces" on the morning news on June 5, 1968. I noted in my journal that night what Hugh Downs had said on the *Today Show*, to explain his repeating the news of Kennedy's being mortally wounded. "We repeat this because so many people are just now waking up—in two different meanings of the phrase." I also recorded a question from a soldier in Vietnam when he heard this news: "What in the hell is going on back there?" What, indeed?

And my own craziness during this period of upheaval, which so greatly affected life on college campuses across the nation, may best be captured in my entry of May 7, 1970: "People all wanting to talk about 'senseless murder' of the four Kent State students in campus riots and circulating inane petitions—lumping together protest of Cambodia, Kent State deaths, trial of Black Panther Bobby Seale, and ROTC on campus. I'm only surprised they don't toss in dining hall food and curfew complaints!"

Scanning through many journals to refresh myself for composing this essay was a bittersweet experience, as doing so helped me relive some beautiful moments as well as some horrific ones, but nevertheless I consider the discipline of recording some reflections on the day just ending as a worthwhile structuring of my life, perhaps most especially because it forces me to acknowledge the value of what others might consider the mundane and the ordinary. I believe that's a good thing.

On Giving and Getting

On the one hand, material gifts have never been particularly important to me. Surely this is the result, in part, of my having been born during the Great Depression and experiencing childhood during the World War II. I recall the thrill of using a large safety pin to attach one of my mother's nylons to the back of the sofa so that Santa could fill it with tasty treats and small gifts. That they were mostly oranges, apples, peppermint canes, pecans, a few walnuts, and the almost-impossible-to-open Brazil nuts didn't disappoint me. In the bottom of the hose, near the toe, I usually discovered a piece of jewelry from Woolworth's Five and Dime, sometimes a tiny necklace with my birthstone, the garnet, and usually the chain didn't stain my little chubby neck green until the second or even third wearing.

We didn't own a nutcracker, so the family shared Daddy's pliers, and I didn't realize until years later that we never called the hard-shelled Brazil nuts by that name, but used, instead, a dreadful racist epithet. (Have I already noted in these columns that the "good old days" really weren't?)

On the other hand, I have pretty much always had everything I wanted, partly because my upbringing did not encourage acquisitiveness. Some friend gave me a coaster on which I place my coffee mug each morning on my desk as I attack whatever's awaiting me on my MacBook Pro. That coaster's message: "Happiness is wanting what you have."

Gift giving and receiving is, therefore, a challenge for me. I have a hall closet crammed with objects I've received from loving friends and family, and I intend to regift most of them—many to the rummage store that supports the Hill Country Animal League. And, in my obnoxious way, I inform most who give gifts to me that "I really don't need anything, but here are some nonprofits I would love for you to donate to in my honor."

I even tried for years to browbeat my loved ones into letting me do the same for them, and I've written several checks to Young Life in Nashville, Calvary Baptist Church in Henderson, Texas, and the Good Shepherd Medical Center in Longview.

Eventually, my loved ones rebelled and requested more personal gifts, so I have adjusted and purchase items from Coldwater Creek and Amazon.com. I am slow and set in my ways, but with harassment I come around.

Way back in 1956 I read and admired Erich Fromm's *The Art of Giving*, and, on my birthday in 1970, a Trinity student, Pat Fry (now Godley†), who was a Spur, a campus leader, bright and quite promising, sent me a passage

† Google her—She's one of many alums who bring honor to this institution.

from that book. As the commercialized season for gift giving approaches, what Fromm wrote captures what I really believe about giving. (Bite your tongue and ignore his sexist language.)

> What does one person give to another? He gives of himself, of the most precious he has, he gives of his life. This does not necessarily mean that he sacrifices his life for the other—but that he gives him of that which is alive in him; he gives him of his joy, of his interest, of his understanding, of his knowledge, of his humor, of his sadness—of all expressions and manifestations of that which is alive in him. In thus giving of his life, he enriches the other person, he enhances the other's sense of aliveness by enhancing his own sense of aliveness. He does not give in order to receive; giving is in itself exquisite joy. But in giving he cannot help bringing something to life in the other person, and this which is brought to life reflects back to him.

Being Kind

I title this bimonthly column "The Short List" because I intend as my subject whatever is at the top of my concerns, interests, irritations, despairs, or delights—you get the idea—as I compose the essay.

That being my plan, it shames me to confess that I'll be lying in this first one: my number one concern, interest (see paragraph above), is the acclimation of two young cats from feral to housebound. Right now the new home of Tux and Atticus is my screened back porch, safely separated from my unseemly curious two tame cats, the recently adopted stray part-Schnauzer, and the poodle pack.

After only a bit of careful consideration, I realized reflection on this adventure, fascinating as it is to me, would appeal only to a handful of crazy cat ladies and a few colleagues who get pleasure from scanning whatever I write so they can note errors in grammar and phrasing.

Of course, I don't have any idea what my readership is—if it exists at all—but I'm sure feral cat rescue isn't a hot topic. So I turn to number two on my short list—beginning another academic year.

I've read the first two issues of this student-edited paper, and two articles in particular moved me—Leslie Barrett's "Would You Still Be My Friend?," in which she describes her changed life after contracting Lyme disease which led to Bell's Palsy, and first-year Julie Robinson's comments on "transitional difficulties."

Although there's great disparity in the challenges these two writers explore, they both motivate me to consider one of the qualities which I believe has always been and must always be a fundamental characteristic of members of this community, both the old and the young—the necessity to be kind.

Decades ago I quit lecturing from a podium at the front of the classroom, instructing my students on what they should conclude about our readings—"Erdrich's message here is," "The meaning of this stanza is," "The most memorably drawn character in this novel must be." I began, instead, to lead discussions of the text.

What could be more fun and more challenging, I reasoned, than sitting around a room with a group of other intelligent, articulate people, examining a text—welcoming one another's opinions, agreeing or disagreeing with them in civil discourse? (Okay, rescuing feral cats could, but I promised that was not my topic.)

Leading such sessions and having them go well requires, obviously, a certain level of patience and self-control from both professor and students, so I include in my course policies two admonitions: "In discussions and in critiquing the work of peers, be respectful, civil, and constructive." And "Be attentive and engaged in class. Consider the possibility that occasional hypocrisy is better than rudeness, engagement better than disengagement."

I saw *Mean Girls* long before Lindsay Lohan went awry, and I've read Atwood's *Cat's Eye* more than once, so I know that adolescents can be remarkably snarky, but, gee, here we all are at this remarkable institution—in this supportive community, populated by the intellectually gifted—with a chance for a fresh start. "Fresh" not only in the way we treat others, but also in the way we treat ourselves.

Since many reading this have no earthly idea who I am, I choose to underscore my theme by quoting a few writers whose advice, perhaps, you will heed:

Ms. Anonymous: "Everyone you meet is fighting a battle you know nothing about. Be kind. Always."

The poet Stevie Smith: "I was too far out all my life / and not waving but drowning."

Novelist Hermann Hesse: "It is only important to love the world and to treat ourselves and all beings with love, admiration, and respect."

And, hoping you will take his language in context and not be overly offended, from my all-time favorite, Kurt Vonnegut: "Hello babies. Welcome to earth. It's hot in the summer and cold in the winter. It's round and wet and crowded. At the outside, babies, you've got about a hundred years here. There's only one rule I know of, babies: God damn it, you've got to be kind."

I spent my first full day of work on the Trinity campus on June 15, 1958, so although you might calculate the years and conclude that surely I'm addled, ignore that, risk trusting me simply because I've been here so long, and practice what I preach in my first of this year's short lists.

You won't regret it.

Some of My Favorite Things

Thanksgiving

Thanksgiving's almost here, and it is, very frankly, my favorite holiday of the year. Oh, I like New Year's Day because of the black-eyed peas and the futile annual attempt at resolutions that'll perfect my life. And I enjoy July 4, for I usually travel to Austin and picnic beside Town Lake to hear the "1812 Overture," delight in the fireworks display, and inhale the scent of something that reminds me of alfalfa burning in the crowd around me. Christmas is not my favorite because the family gathering to exchange gifts and gorge ourselves just has not been very meaningful since my mother's passing. But Thanksgiving I adore.

Usually I enjoy this day of rest and reflection at my own home without relatives. I prefer the food for this holiday, so long as I get the largest portions of white meat, thickest slabs of cranberry sauce, the most nut-, celery-, mushroom-filled dressing, and a presentable slice of pumpkin pie with a huge glob of whipped cream. I honor the day always with some time out of doors—a drive in the Hill Country or, if possible, a hike—and I insist on some private time for listening to a range of favorite albums: Bach's Brandenburg concertos, Leontyne Price's *Right as the Rain*, George Harrison's *Extra Texture*, and Dan Fogelberg and Tim Weisberg's *Twin Sons of Different Mothers*.

I am not one, however, who believes in saving up all words of thanks for this one day of the year. As a matter of fact, I've kept a daily (or, more precisely, a nightly) journal for over ten years. I record trivia—menus, my personal movie reviews, and snide remarks about people who were mean to me during the day, but more importantly, for the last several years I've ended each day with a concrete listing of the "happiest moments of this day."

So when Thanksgiving rolls around, as on any other day of the year, I am already predisposed to list quite easily what gives me joy and what I am thankful for. As I scan through the last several month's journals, I rejoice in the minutiae—the recording of quiet, small moments that make up what I consider the happiest parts of my days, the moments for which I am most thankful.

Most of these would bore the college crowd, but I'll give you a simple smattering from the last few weeks: my dog, Tinker's Damn, limping less since her surgery; cooking steaks with friends over a campfire at the land; hiking at Pedernales Falls State Park and not having a heart attack in so doing; seeing *Girlfriends*, *Midnight Express*, *A Wedding*, and *Interiors*; reading Susan Sontag's *I Etcetera*; catching a frightened moth in the dining room and releasing her safely outside; watering my plants; feeling I openly communicated my concern to a distressed student; having my laundry all clean and my clothes ironed for the week ahead; sipping a mug of coffee, cuddling poodles, and scribbling ideas for a *Trinitonian* essay; a class session in which the students have read the assigned material and discussed and shared ideas with some enthusiasm; receiving an unsolicited and unexpected complimentary remark or comment from a student; being summoned by a friend to observe out the window a gorgeous sunset or a busy squirrel.

Disappointed? I guess so. But I wanted to share with you that for me, because of my journal, every day is Thanksgiving, and while what I'm thankful for may well seem boring and creepy to you, it's awfully joyful to me.

Whatever makes you thankful, I hope you have lots of it on this glorious holiday in 1978. Travel safely. Tell a couple of loved ones that they are. Take a few moments to reflect on how good life's been for you lately and come back to the university ready to face the end of the fall semester rested, or, at least, rejuvenated. Take gentle care. Be thankful.

The Oscars

Born and raised in the East Texas piney woods, I think it would certainly be oxymoronic to refer to myself as a "snob." Some friends, alas, refer to me as a "redneck." I have the current calendar from Jeff Foxworthy on my kitchen counter, and I frequently find definitions that do fit me—"You have to move three animals to make the bed," "No one eats lunch with you twice," "Door-to-door salesmen skip your door." As my friend Bob puts it, "You can get the girl out of East Texas, but you can't get East Texas out of the girl."

Although I really doubt that anyone raised in East Texas can be a snob, I nevertheless am quite particular about which fiction I read, which films and sports events I view, which television programs I record, and which students I teach. The choices in these areas do hint of snobbishness. I suspect this comes from my hearing regularly as I was growing up such admonitions as "Anything worth doing is worth doing well" and later posting on my bulletin board (and including in many of my speeches) Carlyle's "Become all you were created capable of being."

So I rarely read a best seller, I have never seen a reality show or even *American Idol*, and, even though occasionally I try to appreciate undergraduates' tastes by renting some movie such as *The Hangover*, I don't usually even see the box-office smash hits. In the summers, at the beach and in the hammock on my porch, I make exceptions for some best sellers—the usually mesmerizing novels of mystery and intrigue from John Sandford, John Grisham, Patricia Cornwell, James Lee Burke, James Patterson, and the late Stieg Larsson.

I read critical reviews of films, television, and literature and make most of my choices influenced by the critics whose judgment I respect. I am far more likely to trust what A. O. Scott writes in the *New York Times* than what the film reviewer for *Entertainment Weekly* says, and, off-putting and challenging as the winners often are, I regularly read and choose for texts the winners of the Pulitzer, Man Booker, PEN/Faulkner, and National Book annual awards as well as those listed by the *New York Times* as Notable Books of the Year.

Put another way, I may not be a snob, but I value excellence and prefer to spend my time and energy on the best in all areas. I don't watch all collegiate or professional football games, but I do watch many play-offs and rarely miss the Super Bowl; I abhor and avoid the Lakers but love and cheer the Spurs. I admire the proficiency of the Olympic competitors and the international tennis matches, but I draw the line, even as I acknowledge these are also superb athletes, at sitting through those less-than-fast-paced baseball games, any golf, boxing, or wrestling matches, and all those fast cars on fast tracks. Not a snob, but not all that consistent either, it seems.

This acknowledgment of my commitment to excellence is, in my view, somewhat hilariously most evident in that I never, ever miss the Oscars. Even before the Academy began to televise the awards ceremony in 1952 when Bob Hope was emcee and I was a high school senior, I stayed up late in night, year after year, listening enraptured to a tiny radio.

I wept when Olivia de Havilland lost Best Actress for *The Snake Pit* (1948) and rejoiced when she won for *The Heiress* (1949). Though a mere child, I already had high standards. I have never recovered from the injustice of Sally Field winning Best Actress instead of my idol, Bette Midler, in 1979 when the Divine Miss M deserved every award for *The Rose.* (I resent this theft so greatly that, even after all these years, I still want that Oscar justly awarded.)

I recognize the clichés and discomforts of this and all awards ceremonies. I know they are downright silly sometimes. I inevitably feel embarrassment for the inarticulate and ungracious acceptance speeches and appalled by the pompous, self-aggrandizing ones. But I recall highlights: that streaker running across the stage in 1974, inspiring actor David Niven, who was a presenter, to observe, "Just think, the only laugh that man will probably ever get is for stripping and showing off his shortcomings." That moment served me well when a Trinity streaker disrupted a Sing Song performance of which I was mistress of ceremonies. I commented, "If you've seen one, you've seen them all."

Candidly, and perhaps most importantly, if I'm staying up late at my advanced age to see the ceremony yet again, my favorites had better win and deliver gracious, articulate acceptance speeches, avoiding the use of "like," "basically," and "you know" as fillers.

Excellence matters. Believing that "anything worth doing is worth doing well" and going for the gold are good things. Since you are a member of this uniquely fine academic community, considered to be among the best and surrounded by the best, go for it—even if some will consider you a snob.

It's worth it.

The Magic of Movies

In spite of rumors to the contrary, I was not alive during the silent film era, and I did not grow up watching *The Perils of Pauline*. But it wasn't much after that period that I began my lifelong love affair with films.

My first memories are not really of full-length feature films but of serials—literally, cliff-hangers and Westerns. Shown on weekends and terribly effective in drawing the adolescents back for next week's installment, my favorites starred Randolph Scott or Sunset Carson until my affections switched almost totally to the Tarzan films featuring Johnny Weissmuller.

In outdoor play, I organized my neighborhood pals and assigned roles: I was always Tarzan, but the characters of Jane, Boy, and Cheetah would go to friends of whichever gender I chose to assign that day. We were able to shimmy up trees in a grove and swing back and forth, moving from tree to tree. Not exactly flying through the forest on remarkably strong grapevines, as my hero did, but pretty wonderful.

I thought Gene Autry was corny and sang too much, but I admired the more handsome Roy Rogers and laughed uproariously at the antics of his sidekick, Gabby Hayes. As I recall, though sometimes Roy had to rescue Dale, she was occasionally pretty resilient and took care of herself, and I liked that. All these features ended with a duet by the two stars accompanied by the Sons of the Pioneers, and then Roy and Dale, on their lovely, brilliantly trained horses (Trigger and Buttermilk), rode off into the sunset. I never knew what happened in that sunset, but I felt sure it was swell.

At some period in my childhood, a Grissom family tradition was to attend the matinee at the Esquire Theater after church on Sundays and lunch at home. (Sunday was also the only day we had meat, usually the carcass of an unfortunate chicken whose neck I sometimes had to witness my mother wringing in our backyard.)

In spite of the humiliation and embarrassment of my father's inevitably hawking and then spitting both on his way into the sanctuary and later into the theater, I cherished these family outings for years.

Then, one spring, having memorized 250 Bible verses, I "won" attendance at a church camp, where my happiness and confidence were shattered as the pastor used the prop of fizzing Alka-Seltzer in a glass of water to illustrate what happens after death to people who sin— including the sin of going to a movie on the Lord's Day.

The horror of that cruel image and preachment haunts me to this day. Alas, I don't recall my parents' reaction, but I do know that I continue to take the risk of viewing films in theaters and programs on television every day of the week, and I have an engrained distrust of church camps and ministerial authority.

My teenage years were a period in which I spent most of my allowance on movie magazines and adorned my bedroom walls with portraits of my favorite stars. I wrote many fan letters and received in response "autographed" pictures from the celebrities. I even carried wallet-sized headshots of both John Derek and Cornell Wilde, as if they were close friends or relatives. (Today my maturity and sophistication are reflected in my "Bette Midler Gallery," which dominates the walls of my study. Many of these posters and portraits *are* autographed, and perhaps my favorite reads, "For Dean Grissom—with aloha and many thanks for all you've done for us all, Bette Midler.")

In the late 1940s and early 1950s, my viewing pleasures often coincided with my reading. Books that fascinated me—those by Daphne du Maurier, Lloyd C. Douglas, Frank Yerby, Thomas B. Costain—were often made into movies, so I rejoiced in considering them in both interpretations. Just think, *The Foxes of Harrow*, *The Big Fisherman*, *The Robe*, *The Silver Chalice*, *The Saracen Blade*, *Rebecca*, *My Cousin Rachel*, *Jamaica Inn*—read and then seen in the theater with surprising and often disappointing changes made, I soon realized, to please nonreaders!

Nevertheless, to hear lines I'd memorized from these fascinating escapes from the humdrum life of a teenager in the piney woods spoken by great actors or a godlike voice-over always thrilled me.

In my extended "Lloyd C. Douglas is the world's greatest novelist" phase, I mouthed (or, at the very least, recognized) the words from his novels when the actor uttered them in the films: "Last night in a dream I saw the King. He was standing on a high hill, gazing entreatingly into the far distance, across the mountains, plains, and seas. I heard him saying, in sorrow, 'You would not come unto me that you might have life.'" And I wept during *The Agony and the Ecstasy*, as "he felt his soul leave his body, rise upward into the dome, becoming part of it: part of space, of time, of heaven, and of God." Less dramatic, I suppose, but equally impressive were lines from Zane Grey films and books that I felt deserved memorization because of their psychological astuteness, such as "Ah . . . but, Jim, in my fury I discovered my love!"

But after I slowly moved beyond these novelists and discovered du Maurier, both films and novels obsessed me. How could they not, with such writing as "They used to hang men at 4 Turnings in the old days." And the scene from her short story "Don't Look Now," also a brilliant film: "The creature was gibbering in its corner. The hammering and the voices and the barking dog grew fainter, and, oh, God, he thought, what a bloody silly way to die." (I hereby apologize for that spoiler and warn readers there are several more to come.) Or that remarkable opening line of *Rebecca*: "Last night I dreamt I went to Manderley again."

Similarly, during my adolescence books I read in appreciation for their humor were often "translated" into popular movies. I especially love (and still relish re-viewing) *Auntie Mame* and seek occasions in which I can quote my two favorite lines from the author Patrick Dennis: "I always start writing with a clean piece of paper and a dirty mind" and, more useful, "Life is a banquet and most poor sons of bitches are starving to death."

During my high school and undergraduate years, like many others of my era, I fell in love with romantic, gorgeously colorful Hollywood musicals. Easily star-struck as I was, I *think* I realized these films made little effort to capture reality—I'd never seen anyone break into song in the middle of a conversation. But these were influential cinematic experiences, and sometimes, even now, I wish for the beauty and escape of such masterpieces as *Camelot*, *My Fair Lady*, *The King and I*, *The Sound of Music*, *Carousel*, *Oliver*, and *South Pacific*. I even miss the likes of *Dirty Dancing*, *Saturday Night Fever*, and *Singing in the Rain*. It never surprises me that "revivals" of these and other musicals still thrive on the Broadway stage as well as with local and regional theaters.

Although my determination, as an adult, of what turns a film into a favorite is hard to pin down—I appreciate superb acting, cinematography, special effects, pacing, suspense/tension, verisimilitude, all the usual qualities—I also seem to place a high value on good writing in the films I most often recommend to others. I marvel at succinct lines that startle me with their insights, their capturing of a life truth, their hilarious incongruity.

Glenda Jackson delivers Penelope Gilliant's observation from *Sunday, Bloody Sunday*, a line that occurs to me perhaps too often, "Sometimes half a loaf is not better than no loaf at all."

Woody Allen offers too many truths to include, but whoever can ignore "The most beautiful words in the English language aren't 'I love you,' but 'It's benign.'" And "It's not that I'm afraid to die. I just don't want to be there when it happens."

The young Robert de Niro, in *Bang the Drum Slowly*, utters this bit of wisdom: "Probably everybody'd be nice to you if they knew you were dying." But his friend responds, "Everybody knows everybody's dying. That's why people are as good as they are."

Of course, with my well-known—if not always appreciated—sense of humor and appreciation of the absurd, many of the films I admire the most offer one-liners that amuse me in or out of context: Cloris Leachman in *Young Frankenstein* uttering, "He vas my boyfriend." Bette Midler in *Ruthless People* shrieking, "Do I understand this correctly? I've been marked down? I've been kidnapped by K-Mart!" And the incomparable Judy Parfitt as Vera in the film of Stephen King's "Delores Claiborne": "Sometimes being a bitch is the only thing a woman has to hold on to."

Since I was never a popular girl with the boys (really, who could expect any self-respecting East Texas boy to find attractive a chubby girl destined to be both valedictorian and "most witty" in the Carthage High School Class of 1952?), my understanding of "living happily ever after" came mostly from films and books. But neither was completely satisfactory or explanatory. Even D. H. Lawrence in *Lady Chatterley's Lover* confuses and baffles with "She gave herself to him." Huh?

Roy and Dale rode off side by side on their horses— today's Cialis commercials with the man and woman in separate, side-by-side tubs seem reminiscent of these films' conclusions—also baffling. Cary Grant wrapped Grace Kelly, Deborah Kerr, Eva Marie Saint (one at a time, of course) in his arms, as the camera lens panned to fireworks exploding in the sky.

Finally, though certainly not as graphic or specific as what's available in today's films, television, or websites, during my adult years my reading and film viewing has occasionally made me regret being an old maid.

Each filmgoer surely has his or her own memories of scenes of such passion. Mine include not only those of the Grant era (especially *North by Northwest* and *To Catch a Thief*) but also the film version of Daphne du Maurier's *Don't Look Now*, which offers an unforgettable (and shocking for its time, 1973) bedroom scene with Donald Sutherland and Julie Christie, and who could ever forget Kathleen Turner and William Hurt in *Body Heat*?

Dirty Dancing provided more fodder for resenting my marital status, as did *A History of Violence* with Viggo

Mortensen and Maria Bello on a staircase, of all places! *No Way Out* put Kevin Costner and Sean Young in a taxi ride like none I've ever experienced, and Jon Voight and Jane Fonda in *Coming Home* created an erotic and beautifully moving sexual moment.

Movies not only provided most of my vicarious sexual adventures, but they also through the decades—until I became hooked on *Dexter* and *Criminal Minds*—taught me more than I wanted to know about sheer terror. I like to tell people that I appreciate scary films and television programs and read many murder mysteries because in most of them, ultimately, "good triumphs over evil." My friends don't always seem to believe this and choose to think I just enjoy gore.

I still recall vividly terrifying film moments, many of which I haven't seen in decades: when Simone Signoret reacts to seeing the husband she thought she'd drowned rise from the bathtub's water in *Diabolique*, and when Glenn Close, as Alex Forrest, performs a similar moment of horrifying surprise toward the end of *Fatal Attraction*. There's also the power of scenes in which violence is left to the imagination, as when Burt Lancaster calls his wife's bedside telephone and hears a man answer, "Sorry, wrong number," in the film by that title.

But nicely, often stylized to stick in the memory, haunting acts occur throughout my movie history— almost any scene in *The Lodger* as Laird Cregar murders yet another woman and a light fixture's swinging casts eerie shadows on the wall; the reflection of the strangling of Miriam in her eyeglasses' lens as the sounds of a carefree carnival fill the background in *Strangers on a Train*. And who my age didn't switch for a while from refreshing showers to hot baths after Hitchcock's *Psycho*? But then we remembered or viewed *Diabolique* or *Fatal Attraction* and wondered if we should just stick to sponge baths.

Thankfully, my life has, so far, been devoid of personal encounters with violence, and perhaps the vicarious enjoyment of it in reading and film viewing is a safe escape, but not necessarily a healthy one. The fact that I recall so many such scenes so specifically after many, many years should tell me something.

Since I pride myself on noting even subtle foreshadowing, perhaps my favorites are those moments that took me by surprise. In *The Conversation*, just as Gene Hackman is about to give up his search for evidence of a crime, he flushes the commode and bright red blood bubbles up. Michael Caine surprisingly and appallingly switches from Elliott to Bobbi in an elevator, much to my dismay and that of his victim, Liz, played by Nancy Allen. That awful moment toward the conclusion of *Carrie* when I am finally relaxed as Sue (Amy Irving) visits the plot where Carrie's home once was, and Carrie's (Sissy Spacek) hand reaches up from the grave to grab Sue's wrist! Ralph Fiennes as SS Lieutenant Amon Goeth simply scans the crowd below his balcony in *Schindler's List*, then aims his rifle at a little Jewish girl in the one splash of color in the scene, and shoots her. And just when I (and most in the audience) are feeling hopeful that Executive Officer Kane (John Hurt) will be saved from his injuries in *Alien*, that hideous alien creature bursts from his chest!

Even though I had read the du Maurier story "Don't Look Now," the movie scene in which Donald Sutherland corners a little figure that he thinks is his missing daughter, alive and wearing a red cape, is a recurring image of unexpected but foreshadowed horror. Still, in the magic of movies for vicarious experiencing of dreadful, horrific moments, probably nothing captures this more effectively, because of the combination of everything important in cinema—acting, pacing, writing, filming, music, cinematography—than the entirety of *The Silence of the Lambs*.

Recalling and cherishing as I do many brilliant films noted for all the qualities that result in excellent cinema, my mini-obsession also extends to being able to rattle off—as I ask my students to do frequently after reading a series of novels—the characters I would like to have as a friend and those I hope never, ever to meet.

Since I'm such a fan of "good eventually triumphs over evil," it should come as no surprise that those characters I hope never to meet include Mrs. Danvers (*Rebecca*), Bill Sikes (*Oliver*), Hannibal Lecter (*The Silence of the Lambs*), Annie Wilkes (*Misery*), Alex Forrest (*Fatal Attraction*), Anton Chigurh (*No Country for Old Men*), or even Rhonda Penmark (*The Bad Seed*).

All these are memorable for the evil they portray so vividly that I don't believe readers will even have to bother to Google their names to recall them!

Interestingly, the characters from my movie favorites that I'd most like to have as friends are quite often children portrayed by unforgettable child actors—Elizabeth Taylor as Velvet Brown in *National Velvet*, Tatum O'Neal as Addie Loggins in that brilliant film *Paper Moon*, Henry Thomas as Elliott in *E.T.*, Mary Badham as Scout in *To Kill a Mockingbird*, Mark Lester as Oliver in the film of the same name, and Lindsay Lohan as Hallie Parker/Annie James in *The Parent Trap*. What does it say about me that these child actors I most vividly recall with such admiration experienced such difficult lives as adults? I think my favorite passage from Salinger's *The Catcher in the Rye*, in which Holden Caulfield comments on his dream of saving little children before they fall over the edge of a cliff, explains my nostalgia and my lifelong wish to help others avoid the loss of innocence.

Fine and not-so-fine films have enriched my life, contributed to my development of values, and provided healthy and unhealthy escape and distractions from the vicissitudes of life. Embarrassing though it is to admit, I really love the "magic of movies" and always have.

Hero Worship and Role Models

Bizarre as it always seems to me, occasionally someone (most often a woman or young female adult) says to me, "You are my hero." Obviously, I find this perplexing yet flattering, and ask myself, "What in the world could she mean by that?" Candidly, I wonder if the generous person means "role model" instead of "hero," but whichever is intended, the reason for the distinction remains baffling.

Here are some of my guesses: I am way beyond the usual retirement age but still working full-time. More confusing than that, I sincerely and frequently state, "I do what I love and love what I do." I seem to have survived many decades of rampant sexism without too much overt bitterness, regret, or resentment. (I comfort myself by believing firmly that the sexists I've encountered along the way will burn in hell. What could be more comforting than that conviction?)

But maybe the label is a comment on my having remained single in a heavily married—if not always happily married—society, and not seeming bitter about that. I have always celebrated being unwed, and, to be fair, I bet there are a couple of male acquaintances from years past who also celebrate not having wed me.

Perhaps it's my abiding humor that earns me the accolade of hero or role model? Cleaning up the infamous line of my idol, Bette Midler, "Phooey on them if they can't take a joke," I do somehow in most situations—sooner or later—manage to focus on the ironic, the amusing, the paradoxical. On my desk, there really is a tile salvaged from one of the many renovations of the student center, and on that tile is printed one of my frequently uttered mottos: "Shit happens. You deal."

Maybe the reason some compliment so generously is that I remain, without going stark raving mad, proudly a "between you and me" person in a "between you and I" world. I falter way too often in my faith in the perfectibility of humankind, but I persevere in trying to encourage the best. For me, that includes using correct grammar. That's somewhat heroic these days.

Throughout my life, I have tended to have real heroes, many of whom exhibited qualities I admired and to which I aspired. As a child, I placed my father at the top of all such lists because he appeared to be able to do everything; he was dependable, could be counted upon. This stood out to me as an important quality. I saw it also in the stars of the films of that era—almost always men (white men, of course) who solved all problems, defeated all wrongdoers, and made sure good triumphed over evil. Initially, I convinced myself that many of these men resembled my father—Randolph Scott, Gary Cooper—but I expanded my lists of heroic characters to include others who triumphed over evil but didn't at all resemble anyone I knew.

It's hard at my age to recall precisely what common denominators—if any—these celebrities possessed, but I think they were always nicely one-dimensional, without any significant character flaws, and they were always "the good guys." Johnny Weissmuller and Gregory Peck were on that list for decades.

As a youngster I did eventually consider film heroes as role models, and, finally, there were some women (all white yet again). I admired the considerable talent of Esther Williams, more as an athlete than an actress, and the acting of Olivia de Havilland, who played roles of not particularly attractive women, but strong, persevering ones. I liked that.

And, happily, during this same period and in my undergraduate years, female teachers won my admiration—sometimes my adoration—by being intelligent, articulate, compassionate, organized, demanding, all qualities to which I aspired. Interestingly, the most memorable ones were two English teachers in high school, Betty Pearson and Nancy Ruth Carrigan, who possessed the qualities that impressed me and who, significantly, thought I was bright, witty, and wrote well! Role models indeed. As it happens, neither of them was married when they were my teachers, nor was the hero, role model, and mentor of my undergraduate years, Margaret Berry. It was Dr. Berry who encouraged me to apply for a fellowship to Syracuse University's student dean program, and attending that two-year program changed my life in many positive ways. These real-life heroes helped me develop a sense of self and appreciate both my potential and my responsibilities.

As a "mature adult," I suppose one should move beyond having heroes and perhaps even role models, but I continue to latch on to actors, performers, politicians, educators whose concerns for the betterment of humankind I share and whose skills I admire and try to emulate. Like my early heroes, they are all intelligent, articulate, compassionate, organized, demanding. They all speak well and write well. Perhaps most importantly among their admirable role modeling, heroic qualities, these men and women are kind, compassionate, and often downright selfless.

Unlike heroes of my childhood and adolescence, these later heroes clearly have some flaws, but even those failings of which I'm aware do not dissuade me from being an adoring fan and admirer. Finally, and thankfully, women and at least a couple of people of color now get their due.

Among those role models even now, I list educators who built Trinity, James W. Laurie and M. Bruce Thomas; leaders Ann Richards, Barbara Jordan, Hillary Clinton, Gloria Steinem; performers Bette Midler, Meryl Streep,

Helen Mirren; writers Kurt Vonnegut, John Updike, May Sarton, Nora Ephron, Maxine Kumin, Margaret Atwood.

Should people have role models or heroes? Lord knows, I don't know. I do know that admiring certain characteristics and qualities that I see in others and, as far as possible, trying to achieve these high standards in my own life and behaviors seems positive.

Sacraments

Endeavoring to recall scraps of something I read decades ago, the name of a minor actor in an old movie, the closing chapter of a novel I last read when I was an under-graduate—these are some of the so-called signs of aging.

Because I am so compulsive, I rarely misplace items such as car keys, my reading glasses, and my wineglass, but I do occasionally struggle to recall some exact detail that seems important when I want to retrieve it. (The name of the minor actor is usually not a nagging sense of failure, but only because I've learned to verify it via the wonders of the Internet. If I can recall the title of the film or even one of the other actors in it, I can track down the full cast and solve my problem. Who says I'm not a modern woman?)

Much to my chagrin, my first name is Patsy, though I have never used it. Medicare does, and it was an ongoing humiliation to me as a youngster when peers would refer to me as "PG," as in "pregnant." Though none of us had any clear idea what PG was or what caused it, the nickname implied something better left unsaid—something mysterious and maybe even nasty. Ah, those good old days.

Perhaps because of this embarrassment, combined with my adult obsessive ways, I've decided my first name with that initial letter *P* should have been "Persevering."

As that official reminder to count one's blessings— Thanksgiving—approaches, I always, somewhat compulsively, start reflecting on mine, conducting a sort of annual assessment. This year I fixated on some lines I vaguely recalled from Andre Dubus and sought to locate them.

First, I took from the shelves my copy of his 1966 story collection, *Dancing after Hours*, feeling sure the lines were there. Rapid scanning of the pages convinced me that I was wrong. So, as if I were a cartoon character in a comic strip, I slapped myself on the side of my head, muttered, "Eureka," and knew the lines must have been in an essay.

Thanks to the instantaneous response of Amazon's "one-click ordering," I had before me *Meditations from a Movable Chair*, and immediately found these lines I'd been floundering around for: "A sacrament is physical, and within it is God's love; as a sandwich is physical, and nutritious and pleasurable, and within it is love, if someone makes it for you and gives it to you with love."

Dubus's beautifully phrased exploration of the sacraments contends that they are available to us if only we choose to "focus on the essence of what is occurring, rather than on its exterior; its difficulty or beauty, its demands or joy, peace or grief, passion or humor." "This is not," he writes, "a matter of courage or discipline or will: it is a receptive condition."

I realize, as do you, that the more usual definition of sacrament refers to a Christian rite (e.g., baptism or the Eucharist) ordained by Christ and that it is a means of divine grace and a symbol of a spiritual reality; ritual or material elements transmit a sacrament.

At this season of thanksgiving, I'm applying Dubus's broader definition, and I'm directing my perseverance gene toward being receptive to the many sacraments that fill my daily life.

No one would ever want a sandwich I prepared, no matter how lovingly, unless, of course, elegantly slathered mayonnaise and white bread appeal, but I can and do, lovingly and ritualistically, send carefully selected cards of encouragement, compassion, and love; provide for the needs of the furry creatures in my care; prepare prompts and discussion topics to stretch my students and to encourage their critical thinking skills.

And in the classroom I observe my students creating and presenting sacraments to one another, to me, and to themselves as they disagree with peers but state their points assertively yet civilly, as they listen respectfully and attentively to their international peers whose native language is not English, and as, slowly but surely, even the shyest, most reticent ones contribute meaningfully to discussion.

You'll find such examples in your life. Be receptive to them, and don't tell me these are just behaviors, not sacraments. They are gifts and blessings not to be taken lightly or ignored.

Awards Programs

One of the things I love about Trinity is that colleagues as well as students have achieved just about every imaginable distinction—in scholarship and research, in teaching at all levels, in athletic prowess, in theater, art, music, commerce. Even before they graduate, literally hundreds of students receive honors for their scholastic achievements, their leadership, their contributions to improving the quality of life of the campus community and beyond. When I served in Student Affairs, among my greatest joys were chairing the selection committee for Who's Who, advising Alpha Lambda Delta and Mortar Board, and helping select resident assistants.

All this is to say that I *love* awards programs, occasions for presenting accolades, acknowledging the "best of the best"—all those occasions that designate outstanding achievement and excellence. So just imagine my mood when I tell you the Academy Awards approach! Excitement fills the air because I am a nut for awards events, and this one is my all-time favorite. I cannot claim to have listened on radio or watched on television every single presentation ceremony, but the only ones I've missed are the few that occurred prior to my birth and a handful of others that swept by before, as a teenager, I bought a tiny radio.

That I usually haven't even seen all the nominated films or performances has never swayed me from being quite opinionated as to who should win. Loyalty is one of my qualities, so during my years of devotion to Olivia de Havilland, Gary Cooper, and Katherine Hepburn, I was a nervous wreck. That I continue to consider the program a high priority is strange even to me because I have never forgiven and will never forgive the slight to my idol, Bette Midler, when she received the nomination and deserved the Best Actress statue for *The Rose*, and, indeed, the ever inane, banal Sally Field heard her name unjustly called. (It serves her right that she ended up doing osteoporosis commercials while the Divine Miss M "took Vegas" with her *The Showgirl Must Go On*.)

As the 2009 event looms (in red ink on my calendar), again, I've not seen all the films, but I still have opinions: outrage that neither dog (Cosmo in *Beginners* or Uggie in *The Artist*) received a nomination for anything when, clearly, each carried his specific film; though Viola Davis should have won the Supporting Actress award for her brilliant few moments in *Doubt*, now I fear she will defeat the constantly nominated, but rarely chosen, Meryl Streep, for best performance as an actress, and, hysterical as she was in *Bridesmaids*, surely no voter in her or his right mind will give supporting honors to Melissa McCarthy instead of Octavia Spencer for *The Help*. (Parenthetically,

I'm happy that this film has enjoyed success, because I feel guilty about all the caustic marginal notes I made in my copy of the book; please ignore this rhetorical question, but why are best sellers so often poorly written?)

Since I've always been such a rabid film fan, no one who knows me will be surprised to learn that I often whine that there are fewer great achievements in films these days. Oh, sure, the technology permits fascinating digitally enhanced wonders, but it's been a long time since a scene in a movie or lines from one imprinted on me in a lasting way.

I found *The Artist* predictable but admired the audacity of the approach even though the woman next to me in the theater fell so soundly asleep that she snored . . . and during a silent film that's not a great thing. *War Horse* contained all the stereotypes and heavy-handed coincidences of films of yore, but it did take my disdain of barbed wire to a whole new level. *Descendants* couldn't go wrong for me since Clooney appeared in most scenes; I didn't understand *Tree of Life*, but no one else seems to have either, so I'm okay if it takes Best Picture, and, if Brad Pitt wins anything, I'll celebrate.

All this being noted, those nominated for Best Picture of 2011 had absolutely no transcending moment or line of dialogue that I will remember forever. That was not always the case with winners of that highest prize. For example, Deborah Kerr and Burt Lancaster on the beach in *From Here to Eternity*, the singing of "The Rain in Spain" in *My Fair Lady*, the chariot race from *Ben Hur*, Brando's

"I coulda been a contender" speech in *On the Waterfront*, the rescue of the little white poodle in *Silence of the Lambs*, Bette Davis's admonition that many have used (and often misquoted) even if they never saw *All about Eve*—"Fasten your seatbelts; it's going to be a bumpy night." There's Dorothy Michael's "monologue" as she descends the stairs on the soap opera set in *Tootsie*, Albert Finney and Susannah York's dining scene in *Tom Jones*, almost every moment in Spielberg's *Schindler's List*, and a remarkable number of lines as well as scenes in every Woody Allen film.

Movies should, like fine novels, provide something fresh, new, brilliantly phrased that stays with us forever. So with some reservations, I admire the Oscars just as I do honors for superior fiction—the Pulitzer Prizes, the National Book Awards, the PEN/Faulkner, and the Booker. This also explains a primary reason I've served this institution so many decades: we attract gifted students with great potential, and those of us on the faculty and staff do all we can to prepare our graduates to be among the best at what they do. I continue to like having a small role in creating an educational experience that imprints on young adults and serves them well throughout their lives, helping them deserve and achieve distinction.

I realize it's not officially Thanksgiving, but during awards season I can't help but feel thankful.

What You Most Love to Do

Since I never procrastinate, toward the end of semester break I started scribbling ideas for my column. The focus was obvious: the renewal possibilities of a new year. I was proudly ahead of schedule, but now I'm beginning to wonder if procrastinating is not sometimes a good thing.

As I approached the polishing and refining stage of composition, here came the media's alliterative headline "Tragedy in Tucson," and suddenly new concerns competed to be atop my short list. What should I examine: Civil discourse? Gun control? Limiting sales of specific assault rifles and/or their quick-reloading munitions? Reform of policies so that the seriously disturbed can more expediently receive successful interventions and treatments?

Even though lack of expertise or even a dearth of basic information didn't prevent the pundits and politicians from pontificating on these questions and more, I acknowledge that I have no expertise. Since my years on the Trinity student affairs staff, I haven't even kept up with laws regarding involuntary commitment or confidentiality of counseling disclosures.

I am, however, an English teacher, so surely I should be comfortable commenting on the need for civil discourse. Of course, I think we all should possess communication skills that enable us to offer differing perspectives civilly as well as possess the ability to listen to others with almost as much fascination as we listen to ourselves. I don't enjoy confrontation, so my preference is to avoid debate with the disagreeable.

I do, however, yell back at the television screen when someone is offering views that differ from mine. So I don't think I want to explore this too closely. I might wander off into a rant about a certain someone using—either out of ignorance or anti-Semitism (or could it be both?)—the phrase "blood libel." You really don't want me to go there.

I do care about civility and, in my discussion-based classes, insist on civil discourse and constructive criticism. I try to give it, and I encourage my students to do the same.

Sometimes this limits students to such insightful critiques as "That was nice," but at least they don't use sarcasm or vitriol to comment on a peer's work or to eviscerate any assigned prose or any peer's writing or presentations. I'm looking for the glass half-full here.

Beyond reminding us that we should be more civil, I have no solutions for the current sad state of our society, so I return to my original focus on a new semester and new year. My longtime colleague, boss, friend, and mentor Bruce Thomas (yes, there's a residence hall that bears his name) always reminded Trinity students, faculty, and staff of a unique quality of academic life: we get an opportunity with the beginning of each new semester to start all over with a fresh slate. (We have to overlook those pesky *cumulative* grade point averages here, but you get his point.)

We regularly have a chance to get it right or, at least, do it better this time—as a student, as an employee, as a teacher. I have always found this possibility rejuvenating, even exhilarating, and relish a January 1 ritual—listing and considering "10 Things I Most Love to Do." (I suspect that any students reading this may be thinking they rarely have time or opportunity to do what they love to do, but I argue that no matter our age, responsibilities, or commitments, assessing what we value in life and *making* time to engage in those valued activities is essential to our happiness.)

My practice of making this list evolved from a values clarification strategy we used back in the 1960s and 1970s; when I wasn't leading "assertive communication" workshops, I was leading "values clarification" ones. I continue to find this process useful—carefully considering the significant pleasures, even joys, of my life and determining whether or not I've recently done those things, how often I manage to do them, how much they cost. Are others involved? Does packing luggage, standing in lines, submitting to a full-body scan at the airport make the list? Or does stretching out on a comfortable sofa under a good reading lamp, propping a fine novel against Wilbur's[‡] furry little back?

---

‡ Don't get excited. Wilbur is a toy poodle.

If I used clichés, a favorite would be "People don't change—they just get more so." Thus, even though I have many of these annual listings, they don't vary much, year to year. Because I've always been somewhat schizophrenic—often a "public" person making speeches, teaching classes, moderating discussions—I've also always been reclusive, shy, and solitary. My annual lists of favorite things to do reflect these juxtapositions, and surely it's high time I accepted that about myself. Starting the new year—the clean slate—by reviewing ways I am spending my time helps do this.

So as we approach the end of this first month of the new year, I urge you to make your "things I love to do" list, to keep it somewhere readily accessible, and to commit yourself to making certain that you are spending your time and energies focusing on what you value—what makes you happy.

Margaret Storm Jameson observed, "Happiness comes of the capacity to feel deeply, to enjoy simply, to think freely, to risk life, to be needed."

The world continues to be a mess. The very least we can do is try to be happy.

Life Choices and Challenges

The Small Stuff

William Safire memorably stated one of the guides for my speaking and writing: "Avoid clichés like the plague." I eschew clichés, and when I slip and use one, I inevitably misspeak. Nevertheless, "Don't sweat the small stuff, and it's all small stuff" appeals as an essay topic.

Of course, significant losses, disappointments, and setbacks devastate me, but I find myself generally rather resilient in coping partly because I learned long ago that grief never really leaves; the hole created by the absence of a beloved physical presence remains, and I often stumble into it. But so far I have been able to persevere, to cherish precious memories, to acknowledge that nothing ever stays the same, and to appreciate the absurd.

What derails me briefly, despite the "small stuff" cliché's truth, is that very same "small stuff." I like order, routine, ritual; disruptions can throw me off my rhythm. The invention of caller ID and voice mail has been a sanity saver for me; I rarely answer a telephone's ring but instead let the caller record a message and return the call if or when I wish.

Since I sleep with four poodles and sometimes share my pillow with a cat, I can't really claim that my night's rest is always thoroughly refreshing, but there are more disturbing ways to start my day than realizing I could use a few more hours of sleep—for example, I awaken to discover that someone in my bed has been incontinent. Though relieved it wasn't me, determining responsibility is a challenge before coffee.

Once out of the bed on such a morning, the small stuff I face secondly is the freshly produced hairball I discover before putting on my slippers or, once safely in the yard with the dogs, distracting them from what appears to be a dead opossum, lifting the critter onto a shovel, and stumbling to the fence with the body, only to see her or his lips move into a self-satisfied snarl as I toss her or him away. Then, more disturbing early-morning small stuff awaits me in the safety of my electronic world as I find in my spam advertisements for products that will enhance a body part I lack or exceedingly warm greetings from Russian women who must assume I do use that product, do have that body part, and are eager to meet me. Small stuff.

Living as I do in the Hill Country even as I continue to work full-time in the city, I've discovered that many of the minor irritations of my day occur during the commute. The dangers of distracted driving mount with each passing year, but I also try to avoid noticing the critter carnage along the country roads before the interstate, the presence of unsecured dogs in backs of pickups, and the likelihood that the person driving the vehicle in front of me on long stretches of road on which passing is prohibited will never go more than ten miles under the speed limit. (I call these drivers Ma or Pa Kettle.)

Small stuff lurks to irritate me in every mile of driving, it seems. Seeing what I assume are otherwise solid, responsible citizens toss beer cans and McDonalds packaging from their vehicles' windows, tailgating me in their heavy 4x4 trucks, or finding myself behind a huge, heavily loaded truck with a sign attached to its rear—a sign that I assume warns me not to come within 250 feet or risk a broken windshield, but how can I be sure, since the words aren't legible at 251 feet? I talk to myself on these commutes, and I repeat myself: "Do you not have a blinker?" "Get off my tail, you Neanderthal." "Secede? Really? What an idiot."

I avoid huge crowds, standing in long lines, the teensy steps and steep stairs in the mezzanine of the Majestic Theater. I would never consider participating in a midnight sales experience even at Walmart or Best Buy, and for many years, even though there is something to be said for being a part of the "roar of the crowd," I realize I can follow a football game, tennis match, or basketball game better on television than in the stadium or other live venue.

When forced into a crowd at some place like the airport as I await a friend's arrival or when I wander with the mobs at the Southwest School of Art's annual Fiesta Arts Show, I realize that I have turned into a mini-misanthrope. I find myself quoting Jonathan Swift, trying not to comment on the obesity epidemic, holding my breath to avoid inhaling passive smoke, and dreaming of being home.

My abhorrence of large groups of usually large people extends to attending regional fairs. As if parking in what is obviously a pasture and hiking a dusty mile to the "fairgrounds" isn't challenge enough, it doesn't take me long to realize that even though I'm wearing my most casual attire, I am overdressed, which always makes me uncomfortable. Porta-potties have never appealed to me, but cold beer has, so a small-stuff conflict occurs pretty soon after I've made the hike, gotten over my embarrassment about my fancy cargo shorts and tee, and swigged my first beer.

Funnel cakes, fried food of every variety, two-hour performances by clog dancers, and absence of any shade usually motivate me to leave these delights before I've used up all my prepaid beverage tickets. Thus, the final humiliating moments occur as I try to give my leftovers to some child and see the parents staring nervously and accusingly at me as if perhaps I am an overdressed, sweaty pedophile.

Don't sweat the small stuff? Are you kidding me? Doing so adds so much excitement to life!

Dining out as frequently as I do—one of the most telling of my refrigerator magnets reads, "If I can't freeze it, heat it, and eat it, I don't want it"—of course I run into much behavior in other diners and waitpersons that puts me over the edge. Whether it's loud parties at nearby tables, parents ignoring children texting because they too are preoccupied with some electronic device, waitpersons who constantly interrupt conversation at my table to inquire about the meal but then disappear when we need something—these experiences never make my "happiest time of the day" list.

On my class procedures and policies, which I distribute to my students on the first day of a course, I include this: "Be attentive and engaged during class. Consider the possibility that occasional hypocrisy is better than rudeness, engagement better than disengagement." Outside of class I attempt to apply this to my interactions with those whose conduct distresses me. I would never say a word to the person ahead of me in the grocery checkout line who has a large, disorganized collection of coupons to help pay her or /his bill, and, although I almost always go out of my way to say something complimentary to cashiers when I have seen a person ahead of me demean them, I would never speak openly to the rude customer.

The final piece of this argument that attention must be paid to the small stuff: two requests that I hear occasionally set my teeth on edge. Please, reader, memorize these and never say to me, "I hear you're funny. Say something funny," and "What's on your Bucket List?"

I do have an answer for this one: I can't imagine having such a list. I do not procrastinate. I do what I want when I want and almost always have. A longtime motto of mine is "Happiness is wanting what you have." I want to sweat some of the small stuff.

"Companion" Animals

My favorite passage from Tom Robbins's *Even Cowgirls Get the Blues*—in fact, the only passage I recall—reads: "Buffy had every fault known to dog. He was a face-licker and crotch-sniffer, a hair-shedder and corner-crapper, a shoe-chewer and guest-nipper, a garden-digger and cat-intimidator, a nylon-snagger and chair-muddyer, a scrap-beggar and lap-crawler, a car-chaser and shrub-defiler, a bath-hater and air-polluter, a garbage-raider and leg-humper and, moreover, a yapper in that shrill, spoiled, obnoxious yap-style to which poodles alone may lay claim."

Long before I knew these truths about toy poodles, I never envisioned having any pets—certainly not dogs. When I was a child, the family had a series of cats and dogs, most of which stayed only a short while and then, without explanation to us children, disappeared. Certainly they weren't allowed in the house and never received immunizations, medications, "fixing." I don't even know if the pet food industry had begun, and my recollection is that the diet of our pets was table scraps, of which there were few in the Grissom household.

In my personal archives, I have a photo of myself as a very young tow-headed girl wearing a cute dress, sitting in a tiny chair, and holding a kitten. My clasp on the animal could appear to some as if I'm grasping her or him by the neck, but I prefer to think I was just trying to get a good grip for the photo. I do recall two names of my short-lived kittens, Mayonnaise and Silly Billy. I do believe the former was a creamy off-white color, and my recollection of the latter is that she or he was cross-eyed. Much to my shameful memory, my father also had a large, short-haired white mixed-breed which went by an abbreviated racial epithet that started with "n."

"In conclusion," as my students love to say as they come to a premature end of an oral presentation, I certainly had no childhood experience that made me yearn to have any pets of my own. I knew absolutely nothing of the gifts a pet would bring.

As an adolescent, during my high school and college years, my disinterest in having "companion animals" evolved to disdain and revulsion. My late sister, Virginia, first shared her home with an array of Chihuahuas and later with several toy poodles. When I visited her home, in addition to the overpowering smell of accumulated cigarette smoke (Virginia died of throat and tongue cancer) was the competing stench of dog breath, farts, urine, feces. There was no way I would ever consider trying to live in a home with any of those disgusting elements.

The famous lyrics from a William Cowper hymn, "God moves in a mysterious way, His wonders to perform," seem applicable (and not, I hope, irreverent) here. Once upon a time—in 1969, to be more exact—a resident assistant from San Antonio, Gail Wheeler, announced to me that her poodle, She-She, had just delivered a litter, and the Wheeler family (the father, Houston, was Trinity's basketball/golf coach) wanted to offer me the pick of the litter.

Ever polite, I agreed to go by their home on Thelma Drive to see the pups, intending to express my admiration but lack of interest in pet ownership. Then I saw the runt of that litter—a tiny beautiful little creature. I think the phrase I am seeking is, it was love at first sight.

I named her Tinker's Damn, a phrase my mother sometimes used to challenge her children to behave, as in, "You aren't worth a tinker's damn—you are of little significance." Already I was a fan of irony. Tinker's Damn was the most beloved creature in my life for more than a decade, and I continue to include her precious soul in my evening prayers. She was the dog of my life, and her charms completely changed my outlook on life and my list of what brings me joy.

So far, since Tinker's Damn entered my life in 1966, I have shared my home with these dogs: Doodle Bug, Baby Banshee (B.B.), Divine Ms. M (Emmie), Kassandra's Absolutely Fabulous Daughter (Abbe), Teddy, Wilderness Tip (Tippy), Cordillera's Callidora (Callie), Rufus, Eliot (as in George), Wilbur (as in "some pig"), Baby Blanca, and

Wally (as in dumped in a Houston Walmart parking lot). Briefly, after my sister Virginia's death, I had as a companion animal her precious Rudy, about whom a visiting student asked, "Who's the little Nazi with a rod up his ass?" That was Rudy.

In addition to the "faults known to dog" that Robbins describes, my beloved Tinker seemed to thrive on masturbating in front of guests; even when I'd planned ahead and put her stuffed animals upstairs, she would regularly bring them down the stairs so she could pleasure herself in front of whoever.

My most recent generation of poodles adds to the list of faults: the joy of rolling vigorously in whatever smells worst in the yard, and, in spite of my trying every discouragement known to humankind, devouring their own defecation as well as any other dog's or cat's or deer's or opossum's or raccoon's. When I advise visitors, "Don't let them lick you. You never know where their tongues have been," the guests think I'm kidding. I am not. I know.

Are they house-trained? Only when they want to be, although I am assiduous in letting them into one of the two fenced yards many, many times in the day and through the night. Sometimes, as I am learning with aging humans, it's just too hard or inconvenient to wait.

Those pets who have died always seem to have been much too young and much too fundamental to my happiness to leave me—Tinker of heart failure when she was with me on vacation in Ouray, Colorado, Teddy after the veterinarian administered too much anesthesia for neutering surgery, Tippy after some misjudgment was made following a routine dental cleaning, and others of diseases typical of aging—cancerous tumors, kidney failure, diabetes, decrepitude.

I have, in most cases, been with them when they died; on one occasion when the female vet had recommended that a dog be euthanized, she captured the horror and blessing of that experience by asking, "Don't you wish someone loved you this much?" Indeed, I do. I suspect we all do.

Having these companions is, as my longtime vet Thomas Vice put it, "a heartbreak waiting to happen," and thus pieces of my heart have been chipped away with each and every passing. I read the poem "The Rainbow Bridge," and I swear by the Will Rogers line "If there are no dogs in heaven, then, when I die, I want to go where they are" and by the *New Yorker* cartoonist Charles Barsotti's caption on one of his masterpieces, "All dogs go to Heaven, because we're not the ones who screwed up."

When I mention my love of animals in speeches or try to comfort a friend who has lost one, I inevitably share two other quotations: by the poet Maxine Kumin, "How we treat the animals in our keeping defines us as human beings," and by the writer Joy Williams, "The silence of animals heals the wounds human words have caused."

If one needs an explanation for bringing companion animals into a life, those words offer a couple of sound ones.

How I got my dogs, other than the first, my Tinker's Damn, doesn't include many interesting stories—I started looking at the "for sale" classified ads and bought a backyard-bred toy poodle, until I moved to the boonies, was on academic leave, and met a delightful new friend who just happened to have a kennel of purebred toys and lived near me. She convinced me that what I needed was to buy one of hers, put the bitch in the show ring, and develop a new, fascinating hobby.

When Callie completed her circuit of the dog shows and finally attained champion status, I declined to have her continue on the trek to Westminster and said, "Shave the bitch and bring her to me." My plan was to breed her and to sell the pups in hopes of recouping all I had spent on Callie's travels with her handler. The brave little girl bore three males, and all I had to do was raise them for eight weeks before settling them in new homes. Of course, I fell in love, and thus Rufus, Eliot, and Wilbur have stayed by my side, in my bed, and on my lap for the past twelve years.

Most who know me have heard me assert that I have only two regrets in my life so far—that I didn't have a dog until I was thirty-five or a cat until I was fifty-two. That's true.

Here's the entrance of feline love into my life:

One evening when I resided at 138 Oakmont, I attended a dinner in the Great Hall and then was going home to check on the dogs before hiking to Laurie Auditorium to hear Jeane Kirkpatrick. On the way, a little yellowish cat meowed "Save me, save me" from behind some parked cars. I ran into my friend Craig Likness, who was on the library staff and a known cat lover, but he advised me to leave the creature alone and trust that it would be safe.

Dissatisfied with that wisdom, I called my English Department colleague Victoria Aarons, who, although a mere child, was new to Trinity and the owner of a cat. She told me to offer the cat some tuna—to save its life and change mine. All I had was canned salmon, and the loud-voiced cat, which I had in my sexist way assumed was male (I called her Caruso when she should have been Leontyne), brought only joy and beauty into my life for twenty-one years. (Yes, even after she became incontinent, she continued to bring me joy as well as improved skills in house-cleaning.)

When Caruso died I was beyond distraught, and luckily my friend and vet in the city, Tom Vice, had only recently had a kitten dumped at his office. Immediately upon seeing her, I fell in love with Delores de Lago (aka Dorie), who looked like a little jock—gray with white socks—and brought her home. She is an energetic, loving, rambunctious little cat and loves to wake me in the morning, not for food, but for some precious time of stroking and batting her paws while the poodles are still snoring soundly and the "other cat" is in the guest bedroom.

Regarding that "other cat." No number of cats could replace the hole in my life left by Caruso's death, so I was still mourning and verbal about this when the vet technician who had assisted with the euthanizing of Caruso called to check on me. In response to my sadness, she stated—bizarrely, I thought—"What you need is a rag doll." She did not mean a toy; she was a breeder of Rag Doll felines and invited me out to her home in Pipe Creek to see her available kittens.

My friend Sandy Ragan and I made that trip. The sound of large dogs barking outside the house almost discouraged us from knocking, but knock we did, only to stagger from the feline smells that met us when the door opened.

We entered what we readily recognized was a cattery—long-haired, gorgeous cats were everywhere, underfoot, on the furniture, under the furniture. A sheet was stretched across the room, and the breeder announced that behind it were the females who were in heat.

Good to know.

Sandy was muttering, "Select a kitten and let's get the hell out of here," when the door to what we realized was a bedroom opened, and our host's boyfriend came out carrying by the collar "the fox that sleeps in a cage at the foot of our bed."

Sandy repeated her request, I pointed to one fluffy kitten and scribbled a check for $600, and we excused ourselves to hurry home, claiming a prior commitment.

I picked up Princess Prunella, aka Nellie, the next morning at the veterinary clinic and have never returned to Pipe Creek, even though I love this beautiful, blue-eyed, docile, needy, talkative, shedding-each-month-enough-fur-to-weave-a-new-rug cat immeasurably. She personifies sweetness and gentleness.

I think perhaps I've dwelt long enough on the demands and expenses of having companion animals. It's time to summarize what makes all the negative aspects completely insignificant. I really see no "downside," and consider having and loving furry (and finny) creatures in my home one of the most sustaining of blessings.

John Narciso, a psychologist at Trinity for many years, often stated in his speeches that "to trust someone means you can predict his or her behavior." Although it's a wee bit off-putting to define "trust" that way, I think there's truth to it. I trust the cats and dogs in my life; I can predict their behavior, and I know, without a doubt, that when one of them is not behaving as he or she usually does, something is awry: There's a deer (squirrel, opossum, raccoon, dove, snake, stray dog) in the yard. There's a scorpion scurrying across the floor. A thunderstorm is heading this way.

Any unusual presence or change in the weather results in different behavior from the animals. One should never ignore this. If you do, you can expect the scorpion to find the sole of your foot, and you will regret that you don't keep an umbrella in the car.

Most of the time, the unusual and unexpected doesn't happen, and animals love routine and ritual as much as I. OCD, as I tell my students, doesn't quite capture how anal I am, and, frankly, it's a comfort to have seven little four-legged beasts surrounding me who relish—maybe even cherish—routine and repetition. Same time, same place— I serve their dinner, clean the litter boxes, dole out healthy treats, groom the cats, and encourage their exercise by playing with the laser pointer. These repetitive activities organize my life as well as theirs and teach us all patience and consideration. I love this predictability.

I long believed that being a parent required a person to become selfless, to put aside her or his comfort and preferences to care for the child or children, but after observing hundreds of examples of parenting, I'm not so sure about that anymore. As for me, I am certain that having pets since I was thirty-five has given me the gift of thinking of something other than myself much of the time. My first thoughts and actions upon arising involve pet care—letting the dogs into the yard, cleaning litter boxes, replenishing water dishes. I like these activities. I don't expect gratitude, but I do see happy pets.

I've long asserted that except when they're sick and when they die, they only bring me joy, and I think this is true, especially after I realize that sickness often leads to bad behavior; sometimes it takes a while to learn that I don't have a mean dog, but I have a dog with some "psychological" problems. Almost all the time, they really do only bring me joy, including the joy of patience and for-giveness.

Finally, the usual qualities all crazed pet owners list are true. These creatures are intelligent, funny, loyal, loving; they forgive and don't hold grudges; they cherish rituals and ignore imperfections. They keep us humans humble; they make us question whether we really are "superior" in any significant way.

Resourcefulness and Perseverance

Resourcefulness and perseverance have always fascinated me. My father's resourcefulness and perseverance made him heroic in my eyes. For years I was wishy-washy about whether I should emulate those abilities or just be glad I could call on him to make repairs, change a tire, jump-start a battery, solve a geometry problem, assemble a new gadget (which, even then, came with badly translated Taiwanese instructions), or throw a spitball. Sadly, before his death, the only one I really mastered was that illegal spitball, which is harder with a softball than you might think.

Although I've never fully developed my "resourcefulness gene"—I'd rather read a book than clean an aquarium, rather pay for repairs instead of making them myself—I have always been persevering, so much so that sometimes I pretend my first name is Perseverance instead of the dreadfully old-fashioned Patsy.

Perseverance has served me well. It got me through those difficult high school and undergraduate school years, in which I was bright, athletic, studious, and witty but had not blossomed into an East Texas version of Elizabeth

Taylor. Alas, though I persevered far longer than reasonable, I never got close.

Perseverance, combined with my well-honed appreciation of the absurd, helped me survive those decades as the only female administrator—the one receiving less pay and fewer fringe benefits. Nevertheless, I think perhaps I was both wise and resourceful when I just smiled each time a trustee referred to me as "Legs" and asked me to replenish his coffee.

And both perseverance and resourcefulness, along with the slow but steady march of social change, supported all of us who worked for and eventually achieved for Trinity women students the freedoms and responsibilities the men had long enjoyed.

Does today's undergraduate experience help students become more persevering and resourceful? I know that in selecting texts I realize my preference for ones in which admirable characters possess these qualities: the father in Cormac McCarthy's *The Road*, Pvt. John Bartle in Kevin Powers's *The Yellow Birds*, Joe Coutts in Louise Erdrich's *The Round House*, and Zeb, Toby, and their pals in Margaret Atwood's *MaddAddam*, to name just a few.

I also tell everyone I see to view the recent Robert Redford film *All Is Lost*, which may well be, as some critics allege, "a parable of old age" but which is simultaneously one of the most mesmerizing depictions of resourcefulness and perseverance I've ever seen.

A Tovia Smith article on NPR on March 17, 2014, "Does Teaching Kids to Get 'Gritty' Help Them Get Ahead?," addressed a new approach to teach young students "persistence, determination, and resilience"—an effort to assist children in becoming more tenacious by helping them realize that "mistakes and failures are normal parts of learning—*not* reasons to quit."

Although no course labeled Developing Resourcefulness and Perseverance and certainly not one called Developing Grit appears even in the new curriculum, I believe the experiences of life in a residential community with all sorts of diversity (except intellectual ability), the wide range of studies, and the availability and willingness of faculty to assist students in acting imaginatively, solving problems, and overcoming difficulties all combine to enable our students to develop these essential lifelong skills.

In a recent interview, Dr. Thomas Jenkins of Classical Studies expressed a view that I think most faculty hold: we want to help our students develop pathways to knowledge, techniques for finding answers. In other words, we hope to help you become resourceful and persevering.

Whether you are just stumbling toward the end of your first year, a graduating senior, a new employee, or a longtime, wizened one, I hope you'll consider the value of including these qualities in your educational goals.

In Defense of Solitude

Because during the past eighty years I have only infrequently shared my living space with other humans, I realize I've developed some habits, rituals, and behaviors that those who share their homes probably eschew: if, for example, some item—say, the paring knife I religiously use for carving an apple—isn't where I left it, obviously I must accept responsibility for being forgetful. I cannot blame anyone else for this misplaced item.

Clearly, this sort of experience teaches one to accept responsibility for one's actions as well as develop one's memory.

But living alone doesn't only teach good habits: I realize I am both a considerate person and a rather selfish one. I like to do what I want to do when I want to do it—whether that's read a novel, watch a television program, take a brief nap, or enjoy a Jacuzzi bath. I don't like interruptions. I rarely initiate a telephone call because I don't like interrupting others, and I regularly praise the inventor of answering machines. Usually I don't answer a telephone until I hear who's calling, and, embarrassingly, I often stand there listening to some relative or friend asserting, "Coleen, I know you're there. Pick up."

I cherish rituals and spoil myself by only infrequently letting someone interrupt them, many of which involve feeding indoor and outdoor critters (assuming it's proper to label fish "critters"). My daily chores (I prefer the term "rituals") range from cleaning out litter boxes to feeding fish in the cistern and in two indoor aquariums, filling bird feeders in the morning, and providing a small number of appetizers to deer each afternoon.

Though it's hard to write about the pleasures of living alone without realizing that many find the entire topic selfish and off-putting, I've learned to cope with disapproval most of the time. Living alone, I love silence—even though some visitors inevitably note the raucous chorus of cacophonous sounds coming from yapping poodles. The truth is, they don't bark all that much when alone with me.

The sounds that interrupt the silence are, generally, soothing ones—the trickle of the indoor fountain, chimes in the backyard trees blowing in the wind. I rarely have music playing or television on during the day, and I hear no traffic or sounds from neighbors. I cherish this silence.

I do enjoy the—for want of a better term—absence of a necessity to be polite: to repress offense when someone talks through dialogue in a television program or DVD we're viewing; to eat when and what I want to eat and to use whatever level of table manners I wish. Like John McCain, I can blow on my hot soup and can even sip from the bowl if I don't wish to spoon it.

Occasionally, I do reflect that, as my mother would have put it, "You look like something the cat dragged in," and that I could someday become so comfortable with belching, scratching, and farting in private that I'll slip up when in company, but so far I'm not aware of even having the slightest inclination to be that relaxed when with others.

Some aspects of the freedom of living alone are repugnant even to the person herself: not bothering to shower until the end of the day, freely permitting bodily emissions since dogs and cats don't seem to mind unseemly smells or sounds, hiding all bras as far away as possible. It's a good thing I reside in a gated community so that no one just drops by!

I realize there are trade-offs in choosing and relishing aloneness. If I want to share a meal or film, I have to invite others over or accept an invitation; there is no one within the house with whom to discuss the film or program I've just seen or the book I've just finished—but this one is easy to deal with, since I can use the telephone, or, better yet, email to share and to seek critical opinions.

I realize that if I am clumsy and cut myself when carving an apple or if I trip over a poodle as I scurry across the room, I might be better off if someone else were in the house, but so far I'm not anxious about that. I do regularly check in with close friends and know they are nearby and could provide assistance when necessary. (And I do pay a humongous amount monthly to assure long-term health care in the home, thanks to AARP.)

Enjoying my aloneness and treasuring solitude is one thing, but I am afraid that this aspect of my life has recently led me to have one more behavior about which to be critical of others—I am appalled and irritated by the omnipresence of smartphones and the apparent inability of many to be "alone" for even a few minutes. It's everywhere I look: in the halls of the university building between classes as I pass students who used to speak but now have their heads down and their thumbs twitching, in restaurants at tables with others whom they ignore, and, God help us, in the car behind me as I drive nervously along the interstate.

"Cherish your aloneness," I want to shout. Spend your private time thinking, singing along with the radio, planning your next meal, making your grocery shopping list! Don't use the time you could be alone by *always* being in touch with one another.

Yes, because I love my aloneness and solitude, I have to discipline myself not to expect others to share my preferences and not to be critical of those who aren't. Expecting others to share my views is, admittedly, one of my fundamental flaws.

Once upon a time, I came across these lines from D. H. Lawrence which capture so well what I feel about solitude and aloneness: "To be alone is one of life's greatest delights, thinking one's own thoughts, doing one's own little jobs, seeing the world beyond and feeling oneself uninterrupted in the rooted connection with the center of all things."

The Art of Fine Dining

"What's for supper? Push and grits? Push your feet under the table and grit your teeth?" I have no idea how often my father began our meals with this witticism, immediately after he uttered grace at such rapidity that I often wondered if God even understood him. All I know is that's the way most family meals that I recall began, and I'm not sure it ever occurred to me that this must have hurt and saddened my mother, who had spent most of her day planning and preparing those meals. I do think, however, that she laughed merrily and thus was known as a good sport, surely an essential quality for wives.

My mother was a good cook, overweight and suffering from "heart trouble" most of her adult life. Her recipes were challenging to follow or to share—a smidgen of this, a pinch of that—tasting and adding ingredients along the way. Because she was raised in Mexico, dishes of that country were among her best, and when I moved to San Antonio in 1958, I always shopped for pan dulce, masa, and jalapeños to take home to East Texas for her.

Tamale pie, pinto beans, chili were regularly on the menu in our home, as were fresh vegetables (potatoes, squash, tomatoes, okra) from our Victory Garden begun during World War II, and, on Sundays, "fresh" chicken and their eggs from the henhouse in our backyard.

I blame (or credit) the years we lived in Shreveport near the Butterkrust Bakery with my lifelong love of bread, especially hot bread. My mother somehow knew what time of day bread came out of the ovens and would send my little brother and me to the bakery with some change. We would buy a loaf of unsliced bread, hot from the oven, and scurry home with it; then, after my mother put a quarter pound of butter in a cut down the back of the loaf, we devoured chunks of hot bread, no doubt ruining our supper—but not caring.

Because memories of these far-from-healthy meals are mostly pleasant, I still consider—though very, very rarely dare eat—such comfort foods as canned chili, hominy grits, collard greens, yellow squash, corned beef hash, liver and onions. Worse yet, under duress, I will admit to loving fried baloney, cornbread, and black-eyed peas, and my favorite sandwich in the whole wide world is mayonnaise and mustard on two pieces of white bread. Ghastly as these food preferences are, at least I do not include Spam. Even as a child, I realized there was something not quite right about that as one's entrée.

I have little interest in desserts beyond vanilla ice cream, but as a child, I remember licking the stirring spoon as my mother was baking cookies, pies, and cakes, and I recall delicious but rock-heavy donuts sizzling in grease in a big black pot on the range.

Holidays in spring and summer always included homemade ice cream, with the elaborate process of rock salt, men turning the crank on the ice cream maker, and children taking turns sitting atop the machine to keep the freezer steady as the crank turned. Licking the spatula was perhaps even more wonderful than spooning the frozen concoction from the dish.

Then and now, I disdained the placing of mealtime as the controlling event of most days. One meal finished, the children helped clear the table, rinse the dishes, wash them by hand, dry them, and, in what seemed like minutes, start the process of cooking the meal, setting the table, and readying for the next meal.

Probably because I was usually reading a book—sitting in an overstuffed chair, dangling my legs over the side, sucking on a lemon, I resisted my mother's unavoidable call, "Coleen, set the table, please." I always begged, "Let me just finish this chapter." Thus I read rapidly and sometimes cheated. Literature rules. And, thanks to all those sucked lemons, my two incisors are not the originals.

To this day, I cannot tolerate watching family or friends labor over meal planning, preparation, cleanup. Nor am I one who enjoys "lolling" at the table conversing after the meal's been devoured. Friends who delight in lunches or even dinners that last several hours baffle me. It's as if I have places to go and things to do. The "fine art of dining" for me doesn't have much of a leisurely pace.

I've become more tolerant of my own eccentricities as I've aged; I more readily accept that my background and roots never leave. As a friend once observed when he saw me sitting in a purple director's chair from Walmart, waiting for him and his wife in my driveway, "You can get the girl out of East Texas, but you can't get East Texas out of the girl."

Though there was a time in which I laughed at Jeff Foxworthy's illustrations of a Redneck as describing my family and many neighbors, many of his comments, alas, also capture my attitude and life—I do have to "move at least one dog before I can get into bed," I do "talk back to politicians on TV," whenever I roll over in my sleep "a dog (poodle) yelps," and I honestly do consider anything distant from the Kendall county line as "abroad."

These being accurate, it should come as no surprise that my comfort foods include frozen chicken pot pie, tunafish with mayo on white bread, Wolf brand chili without beans, and, always thinking I'm a renegade, a gin martini on the rocks without any vermouth.

A cocktail before fine (or not at all fine) dining and wine with a meal is now a staple of my daily nutritional plan, but this preference developed slowly, starting, no doubt, with the readily available and *free* Royal Crown sodas provided to the family because that bottling company sponsored the Little League baseball team my father coached. When these sodas weren't available, I headed for the Orange Crush or the tiny, cute bottle of Grapette.

Other than a mostly "egg" glass of eggnog at Christmas, alcohol wasn't a presence until my graduate school experiences at Syracuse. It's a wonder I found these pleasurable, because the first choice of my peers—women from Binghamton and New York City—was Mogen David! Then, as now, it seemed to be sweet syrup masquerading as alcohol. To show my gratitude for this sharing of the Yankee culture with me, I offered these new friends tall tales, which they believed, including the claim that, to support the family, my mother sold quilts she'd made depicting the dinosaur tracks in our yard.

I've moved beyond Mogen David; my taste in wine has improved. But I still do, at many dining occasions, as I try to sip and not to gulp my beverage, recite from memory an appalling truth: I drink to make other people more interesting. Shameful but oh so true, I suspect, for many. Since this collection of essays is to be candid and truthful, I might as well admit it.

Even though the restaurants in this region at which I do believe I was served the best-prepared and most delicious meals of my life have mostly closed (La Louisiane, Chez Ardid, Josef's), I do still appreciate the service, elegant surroundings, and beautiful presentation of meals at Las Canarias on the San Antonio River, Silo 1604, and sometimes even the dining room at Cordillera Ranch or the noisy acoustics at Cappy's in Alamo Heights or the Cypress Grill in Boerne.

Nevertheless, my favorite fine-dining experiences these days are old favorites, restaurants not known for elegance, but certainly with an almost perfect record for delicious food, hospitality, and quick in-and-out—meeting my standards: Los Barrios and Sea Island!

At least I didn't add to that list my more usual fast-food pleasures—Bumdoodler's and Dairy Queen in beautiful downtown Boerne. My mother would be appalled!

Getting the Girl Out of East Texas

One cool evening as I waited for my friends Jill and Bob to pick me up for dinner, I decided to save time by waiting for them in my garage. I sat in my purple canvas director's chair from Walmart, and as they drove up, Bob commented, "You can get the girl out of East Texas, but you can't get East Texas out of the girl." Immediately, though appalled, I realized this was a perceptive observation.

Born in Mt. Pleasant, raised there and in Shreveport and Carthage, I left only when I went to college on my full-tuition ($50) valedictorian scholarship at—where else could it have been—East Texas State Teacher's College (now Texas A&M-Commerce). Put another way, East Texas was my influence and my only influence from 1934 to 1955.

Those were the decades of water fountains labeled "colored," which always attracted me, but which my mother dragged me away from. Those were the decades in which no children of color attended my school or church, and, if they came to the Esquire theater, they entered by a different door and could only sit in the balcony.

My parents usually used the term "colored" and referred to the neighborhood where these people lived as being "across the tracks." I did have a "colored" friend, the daughter of the woman who occasionally helped my mother clean house or put up preserves. Even though we played happily together, I still remember clearly and painfully that she and I could not eat our lunches together. I was never given a reason; it just wasn't to be done.

My daddy did use the *n*-word, but he probably didn't think of himself as discriminatory or prejudiced, because he worked with black men and respected them, and he certainly admired black sports figures immensely, though he did credit their athleticism to some genetic quality whites lacked. My mother occasionally went "across the tracks" to help with a childbirth, and she got cruelly criticized for arguing with women in her crocheting club that they should be charitable to those "across the tracks" rather than send money to "suffering natives in Africa."

Even in undergraduate school, I had no black classmates or teachers. When the film *Carmen Jones* debuted in 1954, I drove a group of classmates to Dallas to view it. We had never seen—or even realized—that black people fell in love, had romances, embraced. We had never seen anything like this film, so we stayed to see it twice, thus missing curfew and receiving infractions. It was worth it. Eyes began to open, thanks to Harry Belafonte, Dorothy Dandridge, and Pearl Bailey.

Leaving East Texas—the area as well as the college— for Syracuse University was momentous. I had black classmates and residents in the cottage I supervised; I also had many Jewish students and friends, another population that was nonexistent in East Texas. My sisters both frequently commented, "Ever since Coleen went off to Syracuse, she was never the same." I may still have East Texas in me, but there are also the Syracuse experiences.

There, because of integration, the athletic teams also had black members, and the great Jim Brown, All-American, was leading the Syracuse Orange during my two years of graduate study.

Was it education that "broadened my horizons" and got much of East Texas out of me, or was it just that I got out of East Texas?

San Antonio was not in the piney woods, but when I first moved there in 1958, Trinity University had no black faculty, no acknowledged Jewish faculty, and only a handful of black students. As a head resident, I often took some of the women ("girls," they were called) around town in my car, but whenever our one black student was with us, we had a terrible time locating a café or restaurant that would admit her.

I've only written one letter to the editor of the *San Antonio Express-News*, and that letter concerned the closing of Earl Abel's Restaurant, located for decades at the corner of Broadway and Hildebrand. I wrote to praise that establishment for being the only place anywhere near the Trinity campus where we could all be served. (Inconvenient as the new location of Earl's is, I still dine there occasionally, just out of gratitude.)

Growing up in East Texas in the age of segregation and open discrimination and prejudicial treatment did not ruin my life, nor did it develop prejudicial habits in me. On the contrary, I think I have always tended to overcompensate for the experiences of those years, tending to be kinder and gentler to students of color in my classes, and maybe even subconsciously expecting less of them. I fear that my East Texas background motivates me to bend over backward to help black students, even when they don't need my help at all. That embarrasses and shames me, but I am consciously aware that there's much to be forgiven, and I'm just trying to catch up.

I struggle to keep East Texas out of my life in many other areas. My choices of foods are disturbingly influenced by the temptations of down-home cuisine—fried anything, especially okra, chicken, and fish; barbecue (beef), tamale pie, casseroles made with Velveeta, mayonnaise slathered on everything, pinto and purple-hull peas. If I were to succumb to these tasteful wonders, I guess I would also ultimately add Hamburger Helper, Chef Boyardee, and even Spam.

My vocabulary certainly has "enrichments" that obviously should not be uttered by a recipient of a doctor of philosophy degree. Of course, I use "y'all" and "fixing to." They are both wise and sophisticated to some degree. I also, however, too often say "full as a tick," "going whole hog," and "stubborn as a mule" without having any earthly idea what this animal imagery really means. Can the phrasing be both vivid and murky?

In social settings, at which I am always nervous and anxious, I hear such phrases slipping out of my mouth as "You're sure a sight for sore eyes," "I haven't seen you in a month of Sundays," "It's been a coon's age," and the warmest of welcomes, "Bless your heart." In my intellectual discourse, my most vivid phrasing, usually used to describe the state of the nation or the destruction of this planet, is "heading to hell in a handbasket."

Honestly, since I really do not even know what these terms mean, my reliance on them baffles me, and I can only mutter to myself as I recollect my verbal faux pas, "It's East Texas's fault."

Apparently you can get the girl out of East Texas, but you never, ever get the East Texas influences out of the girl. At least, not this one.

Dealing with Change

Although I don't sing "Auld Lang Syne" or make New Year's resolutions, I am always certainly aware that I need to focus as I write checks or date notes and make sure I've moved the digit to a new year. In addition to the bombardment of listings of best and worst and the boring coverage of mobs of people celebrating in Times Square or at Hemisfair plaza, I remember that we've entered a new year because my birthday falls early in January, and I have to focus on the correct age—I am *not*, as I continue to think initially when asked how old I am—really thirty-five.

Instead of resolutions, on the first day of the new year, I make a list of the things I most love to do, and I examine it closely and rejoice in the blessing of being able to do these favorite things regularly. It probably helps that nowhere on that list is riding in a gondola in Venice or seeing the Mona Lisa at the Louvre.

What I most enjoy, interesting to me if no one else, has changed little in the past few years: I still relish leading discussions of fine literature with articulate, intelligent others; I still love reading a chapter and dozing a chapter on the study sofa with four toy poodles upon my person and a couple of cats occasionally wandering by to assess the quality of my latest read. You may think, how boring! You would be wrong.

I also note that it's a new year because the fall semester's ended, and the spring one lurks. I prepare my little three-by-five cards with ID photos and begin to memorize names of those in my classes. Rosters have changed, so I have three new batches of students to harass about eschewing passive-voice verbs and writing with simplicity, lucidity, and euphony.

Two changes at this turn of the calendar to 2012 make my short list of preoccupations—the salvaging of the usually beautiful campus as construction proceeds on the Center for the Sciences and Innovation—and, since I resided at 138 Oakmont Court for nearly two decades, the administrative decision to convert those university properties to faculty office buildings instead of using them as homes for officers of the university.

I loved the writer May Sarton—more as an interesting person of strong convictions, frankly, than as a brilliant prose or poetry stylist. I have long used some of her lines in my speeches, and they're useful here. Sarton wrote,

> Does anything in nature despair except man? An animal with a foot caught in a trap does not seem to despair. It is too busy trying to survive. It is all closed in to a kind of still, intense waiting. Is this a key? Keep busy with survival. Imitate the trees. Learn to lose in order to recover, and

remember that nothing stays the same for long, not even pain, psychic pain. Sit it out.

Let it all pass. Let it go.

Candidly, I think some animals caught in traps don't react this way at all; we've all read of those that chew off a limb in order to escape, but let's ignore that, because otherwise Sarton's elegantly phrased thoughts and her suggestions on coping with change won't work for this column.

In 1958, when I first came to this campus, it wasn't much lovelier than it is during this construction process, but thanks to the generosity of trustees such as Gretchen Northrup and other benefactors, the gorgeously manicured campus appeared. (Yes, I'm one of those who remembers that there weren't many trees, but Gretchen had her workers dig up small oaks from her Hill Country ranch, haul them to the city on flatbed trucks, and plant them in what used to be a lovers' lane and rock quarry.)

So as the spring semester began, I summoned my ability to focus on change in a positive way and tried not to whine as I wandered around the fence barriers trying to locate access to a door to Northrup Hall, and I used as my mantra: "It will be beautiful again soon. It will be beautiful again soon."

And, sure enough, by the time my classes met for the second session, most fences disappeared, and I believed my mantra worked!

I am trying to do the same with my initial reaction to the different uses of the university properties on Oakmont. When I lived there with only two poodles and one cat, annually I hosted literally hundreds and hundreds of students, faculty and staff colleagues, alums, and parents of students.

I've always been deeply committed to the vitality a sense of community brings to the campus. Though sometimes too exhausted from a hard day at the office dealing with student affairs crises, I truly valued having members of Alpha Lambda Delta and their "favorite professors" picnic in the backyard. Resident assistants and student leaders of various organizations came in and out of my home, developing new friendships and marveling at how much better Aramark cuisine tasted outside of Mabee Hall.

My favorite events, which became traditions, were a celebration following spring commencement, when I served the graduates and their families champagne and popcorn. I delighted in having them depart their undergraduate experience with this example of my culinary skills, and I took much pleasure in creating memories for these young adults I had either loved or endured for four years.

But if this was my favorite annual hosting, the most personally enriching experiences of occupying as my home a university residence adjacent to campus were these two: first, though there weren't many of us in those decades, each year the women of the faculty enjoyed an evening of '70s music blasting from the stereo, great food, good wine to be sipped (or swilled), and sacred time to laugh, gripe, and commiserate with other women in a mostly man's world. These relaxed gatherings helped us bond and develop lifelong collegial relationships outside our specific academic disciplines as well as some deeply personal, long-lasting friendships.

The other primary "benefit" of residing at 138 Oakmont was hosting wine-and-cheese socializing or backyard picnics honoring some of the most influential writers of my lifetime.

This isn't a full list, but just scan it and be astonished at the richness added to the lives of those who were there to chat informally with Susan Sontag, Kurt Vonnegut, Saul Bellow, Joyce Carol Oates, Scott Momaday, Jane Smiley, John Updike, Louise Erdrich, Margaret Atwood—and, yes, even May Sarton.

Surely such gatherings will still occur, but I can't stop myself from wondering if they will be as relaxed and comfortable in the Great Hall or some classroom as they were in a university-owned house lived in and personalized by the administrative staff person who resided there.

To rephrase myself: I acknowledge the inevitability of change (though I'm still trying to wrap my mind around the death of my colleague and friend Bill Breit, and the untimely retirements of two faculty stars—Sarah Burke and Larry Kimmel).

Even at thirty-five—or whatever—I realize that progress cannot occur without change. That being a given,

I focus my reflections on the disturbed campus landscape and the altered use of the Oakmont homes on trusting that the values I consider fundamental to the essence of Trinity University—values evidenced by having magnificently maintained, breathtakingly beautiful environs and the commitment to sustaining a sense of community—will survive, even though they endure and flourish differently.

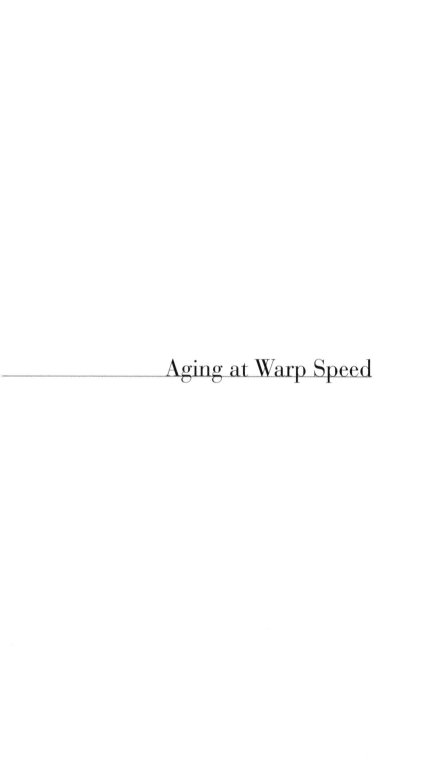

Aging at Warp Speed

Technology

It all began with voice mail. I would come in from a meeting and have many voice mails. It was a whole different way of communicating for me because I like to work one-on-one. Sometimes, as who I am, it's important that I leave messages in my tone of voice with my enunciation. It is easier to do with voice mail than a secretary. If I want to leave a message to be laughed at, I can do that with voice mail. Voice mail has made me more efficient. I can leave a message.

Email has really changed my life and made me a little crazy. I get many, many emails, from students asking about policy exceptions to students asking for recommendations. I am scared to rely solely on email, though. So much of my email is garbage that people think I will find amusing.

TigerTalk has interminable dialogues—I rarely read them. Email is extremely efficient for me.

I do, of course, correct grammar. I write back to my colleagues and inform them of mistakes to shame and humiliate them in a private manner.

The danger of technology has not yet affected me. It's very tempting to fire back something scathing after receiving an email that makes me angry. I worry about people sending things without first reflecting on them.

I find people use email in passive-aggressive ways. Rather than coming in to complain or criticize, they send an email. I would prefer that they come in and feel comfortable to express their concern.

For days I did not have telephone service, so I would stand out on my porch with my cell phone. I don't yet have a fax machine or a computer at my home.

Technology's Creeping Up on Me

It's becoming a habit for me now that 2010 has arrived to hear of some "must have" new convenience and to proclaim, "I'm never getting that."

This attitude began, I think, with the invention of the television remote control. Friends were purchasing this device so they could change television channels, lower or increase volume, turn the set off and on—that sort of nonsense. I announced to anyone who was interested—as well as to many who weren't—that this was a lazy and unnecessary device. The distance to the dials on the television was a short one, and getting up now and then to make changes would be good for all viewers. I would never use a remote.

So for several decades now, I've relied upon a series of remote controls and now rely totally on an expensive model, the Omega Universal Remote, to save me the exertion of moving any muscle beyond those in my right hand throughout an entire evening.

Somewhere along the way, similarly, I donated to a thrift store boxes of 78 rpm vinyl discs with no idea that someday they would be valuable, and I moved to duplicate my library of favorite music, first in 45 rpms, then

8-tracks, then small cassettes, and next, I think, in compact discs. I moved slowly but inevitably from a bright yellow Walkman to a tiny (easy to lose in the bottom of my purse) iPod.

Dragged unwillingly as I am into accepting what appears to be that marketing ploy accurately referred to as "planned obsolescence," so far I have refused to start relying on the iPod and streaming services for all of my music. I may well be the last person on earth still ordering compact discs from Amazon, but I regularly do even though it's never "new" music. I replace long-loved but misplaced favorites, such as *The Best of Linda Ronstadt* and *Graceland*. If I want this music on my iPod, I get some technologically gifted friend to make that transfer for me.

While I suffer and spend much money on these "upgrades," I sometimes wonder about others who must have lost more in this process of changing technology—the Columbia Record Club, for example. Whatever happened to all those people who delighted in sending me some unwanted album before I got around to responding prior to the due date that I didn't wish to order it?

This creeping invasion of electronics in our lives never seems to end. Reading books—the operative word here is "books"—has been an essential part of my life for as long as I can remember. I love the heft, the smell, the feel of a book, and I impress myself regularly by remembering on what side of a page and approximately on what part of the page an admired or detested passage appeared. I love being able to flip around in a book and almost immediately locate such passages.

I spent many hours of my young adulthood, clutching a big, fat volume as I sat in a stuffed chair with my legs hanging over one of the arms, sucking on a lemon and plowing through the riveting prose of Daphne du Maurier, Lloyd C. Douglas, Dashiell Hammett, Irving Stone, and many others. (The necessary replacement of the enamel on my two front incisors was a small price to pay for the joy of those hours. Lemons have never tasted as good since.)

I don't experience such joy in reading so much anymore because, of course, I've followed the "evolving of reading" too. I've purchased several Kindles as they improve in lightness of weight and lighting of screen. My current favorite, because of the small size and light weight of the device combined with the humongous font of which it is capable, is the Kindle Paperwhite. It fits handily in my purse and can be opened conveniently as I await the arrival of a plane bringing a friend home or try to appear patient as I wait in the physician's office.

There must be a way to go to "settings" and prevent the device from putting—in teensy print—how much time remains to finish the book, but I've not bothered to remove that because the very idea of timing the reading of a book, of putting pressure on the reader, of giving casual readers "important" information as to how long it took them to finish a novel, so appalls me. (Was it in *Sweet Tooth* or *Super Sad True Love Story* that this pesky detail occurred?

Wherever it was, I read about it before experiencing it, but I was still cranky when it happened to me.)

One of the advantages of reading from a tablet is that I no longer flop in a big stuffed armchair; instead, I loll on a red leather sofa in my study. In that position I am plastered under poodles, and holding the lighter Kindle above the toy dogs in my lap is much easier on me and them than having to prop a tome such as *Wolf Hall* or even *The Goldfinch* on little Wilbur's back. The poor dog would no doubt be as crooked as Quasimodo if I did that.

When first my students—both the more mature and the undergraduate—began to bring readers to class instead of hardbacks, leading discussion in which I insist on references to precise textual detail was a mini-nightmare. Those without "real books" could never find the correct passage referred to by others with them, and vice versa. Never underestimate the minds at Amazon: quite soon the attention to detail at that mammoth company provided the ability to locate a passage merely by typing in a key word. There went my last argument against permitting electronic readers in class.

Other developments (I refuse to use the term "improvements") in technology abound in my life, of course. The programmable thermostat. I doze off twice a year while standing next to the technician who is instructing me on setting and adjusting the temperature. I walk over to the thermostat and change the temperature with my aging, gnarled fingers. And the cordless telephone with programmable directory and available call waiting. Usually I dial the number I want, and I decline the call-waiting service.

Finally, there's the marvelous iPhone. With my telephone as well as my computer, I do as little as possible. I still keep lists on paper scribbled by hand, and I have only called upon Siri once. She is, as Apple alleges, "an intelligent personal assistant and knowledge navigator," and the directions she gave me were correct, but I couldn't handle the situation. I was unable to accept such graciously presented information without saying, in my own gracious way, thank you and please, throughout the conversation. When I thought about it both at the time and later, this was bizarre. I would rather get lost.

So it is as I approach my dotage. I accept change and promised improvements and conveniences grudgingly and somewhat ungraciously. On the one hand, I fight against my growing dependence upon these technologies; on the other, I can't imagine life without my universal remote, my cell phone, voice mail, my iPod, my three Kindles, or my (really, Trinity's) MacBook Pro.

Such is life for the elderly in the twenty-first century.

Change

Change. Everybody talks about it, but nobody does anything about it.

I've already hinted in one of my previous forays into this role of essayist—if I may use such a respected term so loosely—that there are certain dietary changes necessitated by growing older. But not being able to digest jalapeños is a mild adjustment compared to coping with the mutabilities of the human condition. This past week I was asked by the president of Sigma Tau Delta to read poetry in the Rathskeller at lunch one day—not my own poetry, she wisely specified, but others' poetry that had been or was important to me.

Rereading some of these poems, significant to me during my adolescence, reemphasized my long years of fretting over change and my constant struggle to learn to face it with great equanimity.

For one, I pondered Edna St. Vincent Millay's "Childhood Is the Kingdom Where Nobody Dies," and I acknowledged the painful truth of some of her lines, such as "Nobody that matters, that is. Distant relatives of course die, whom one never has seen or has seen for an hour." But as Millay warns, childhood is over when closer ones die.

Like the "friends" of the deceased Ivan Ilyich, we're first relieved that it wasn't us who died, but then, when we feel safe for a few moments, we mourn his passing. For me, at first the deaths were those of beloved teachers, older colleagues, the genius administrator who built this institution, a couple of college classmates, and then, the one I suffered most keenly, that of my delightful mother. Change in our lives occurs so often without foreshadowing, as we say in English 320, and we have so little, if any, control over most change, that I'm not surprised I've spent so many wasteful hours anguishing over it.

Suffice it to say that change doesn't occur just with physical death. It happens, of course, in a myriad of other ways. We love someone for a while, and then we don't. We are in the foreground of someone's horizon, nurtured and cherished, and then gradually, or suddenly, we're removed or replaced. And in each instance we are changed.

We have certain skills and abilities, and then they atrophy. For a while, in my life, I could recognize any Beethoven symphony by hearing only a few passages from any movement. Now I have to stop and debate whether it's Bach or Mozart, a piano or a harp. I don't devote the time to music I once did. In 1953 my bedroom wall was plastered with clipped photos of movie stars, and I could name the actor who played the maid or the desk clerk in any pre-1950 film and tell you who they grew up to be. Now I have trouble distinguishing John Travolta from Jacquelyn Bisset. That's change too.

I don't wish to whine, because I like what's happening in my life right now. And most of the time I am able to apply Viktor Frankl's wisdom that the only freedom change cannot revoke is the uniquely human capacity to decide how to respond to it.

For myself, I'll hope to heed David Zaroff. After all, haven't you heard me quote his statement that college students grow from dealing with administrators who behave with "restraint and expressiveness"? I may not always manage it, but I'll surely give it a good try.

Clichés

I abhor clichés, endeavor not to use them and shame my students who do, even though I grew up with such memorable lines as "sleep tight, don't let the bed bugs bite," which lately might be a propitious bedtime admonition. As a teenager in East Texas, I regularly used the revolting cliché "full as a tick" after I'd cleaned my plate of collard greens, fried okra, mashed potatoes slathered with margarine, and pinto beans—the substitute for unaffordable meat. My father often asked at such meals, "Is this another push and grits supper?"—as in, push your feet under the table and grit your teeth. I know the power of the cliché.

Even today, I frequently announce at the end of classes, "God willing and the creeks don't rise, I'll see you Tuesday [or Thursday]." How confusing this line is. I never know, even by "doing research," as my first-year students call "Googling," whether it means "creek" as in body of water or "Creeks" as in a tribe of Native Americans. I really must check into that.

I hate clichés, I really do. Nevertheless, I think I've recently invented what promises to be a fabulous one and am proud of it. It is this: "iPhone, iPod, iPad—therefore,

I am." Cute, huh? I find myself working this clever observation into conversations in a feeble effort to convince others that I am a modern woman, technologically skilled. Of course, there are degrees of modern. I don't belong to Facebook and deliberately do no tweeting, texting, sexting, or even twiddling.

Matt Richtel's article in the August 25, 2010, *New York Times*, "Digital Devices Deprive Brain of Needed Down Time," shattered my already shaky pride in my cliché. He criticized multitasking and motivated me to consider what I lose, along with what I gain, through my obsession with electronic devices.

For example, I've spent five decades trudging up the stairs of Northrup Hall (which has many more stairs now that I am old than it did when I was young—what's that about?), and greeting students and colleagues has always been a delight—exchanging salutations, offering some snide observation on recent campus gossip, commenting insightfully on the weather (e.g., "Hot enough for you?").

Those days and exchanges seem to be gone. Rarely does anyone even make eye contact; eyes glued to a cell phone, my fellow campus citizens are either thumbing away on the keyboard or talking into the device. If they aren't busy with their phone, alas, they have their ears plugged with little buds, obviously transported by something such as Beethoven's "Egmont Overture" and incapable of speech.

I wander around outside on campus less than I once did, but I suspect the situation is the same. Obsessed with their digital devices, some campus citizens don't rest their brains. They don't listen to the sounds or even notice the beauty of this environment—fountains, waterfalls, acequias, squirrels scampering in the live oak branches, and cats purring in gratitude for the good lives they enjoy, thanks to the CAT Alliance.

When I finish teaching, I deliberately postpone resting my brain for a while as I head home and face the I-10 challenge of avoiding and being avoided by intimidating Dodge Rams and Ford Raptors.

But when I reach my home—let's be honest here—there are compact discs, high-definition televisions, DVRs, computers, DVDs, and all those "i" items. But there is also silence, except for the rejuvenating sounds of fountains splashing, windmill turning, birds celebrating being alive, and, oh, yes, yapping poodles and meowing cats.

Do read Richtel's article, reflect on the wisdom of his views on the brain's need for some down time, and find ways to get it. Even in this fascinating, almost appallingly appealing digital world, I think we can do this and even manage to experience more face-to-face conversations, focused eye contact, and acknowledgment of our shared humanity. Maybe we could even speak to one another sometimes as we pass on the stairs. Maybe I could even invent a less troubling cliché.

I've Been Sick

Off and on for the past several months, I've been sick. Since, as I approach my eightieth birthday, I have rarely been ill and never seriously so, lately I've often been in a panic and a funk. Doomsday mentality dominates.

Certainly, I've undergone the health-related challenges that seem inevitable for anyone who reaches my "ripe old age"—cataract removal, uterus/ovary removal, demeaning colonoscopies every few years—but I still have my tonsils and appendix, have never broken a bone, and have never received a life-threatening diagnosis. So even I wonder: how dare I whine when I have sinus/bronchitis problems now?

Perhaps it's just the unfamiliarity of not feeling well. Perhaps it's the embarrassing accoutrements of this particular ailment—shortness of breath, gasping for air, incessant hacking cough (which sometimes, alas, initiates an unexpected response at the other end of the alimentary tract), wheezing, and, most humiliating of all, thanks partly to the effectiveness of Mucinex, the overwhelming and frequent need to spit.

When I was a child, one of the horrors of my life was my father's loud hacking and spitting. He did it out the car window, so that my brother and I, riding in the backseat, learned the hard way to duck to the car floor when we heard the sound. (Some readers won't even understand this, but there was a time when cars weren't air-conditioned, and cranking the windows down for air was a necessity.) Daddy's habit, however, was most appalling to me because he almost always performed a ritual as we joined him outside the church to enter the sanctuary; inevitably, he cleared his throat and expelled a glob that was relieving to him and dreaded by me. Now I better understand his need and emulate his habit—but at least I do it in private!

My affliction, while not serious or particularly embarrassing because I avoid social engagements, is creating quite an interesting history. I consulted an allergist, who, after subjecting me to the skin test, politely informed me that "as we grow older, this test isn't very accurate" and referred me to a lab to have blood drawn. The blood test revealed a most surprising (make that unbelievable) diagnosis: no allergies.

Really? I sneeze, cough, and spit off and on every single day, and these delights aren't caused by allergies?

Ever compliant to the judgments of experts, I went next to the Texas Sinus Center and underwent several CT scans of my sinuses, followed by regimens of antibiotics and steroids. When I continued to deal ineffectually with my affliction, I finally turned to my general practitioner, knowing she treats "the whole person," and received a diagnosis of "acute bronchitis," although, as I wittily remarked to my students, "There's nothing cute about it."

Antibiotics and steroids snapped me into shape for a while, but one can't stay on these too long, so I've spent the holiday season breathing through a nebulizer and puffing on two different inhalers. I am not a happy camper.

What I do is take the opposite from positive approach to these treatments; instead of focusing on realizing I do feel even a bit better, I decide I will never ever feel well. I make lists of things I will never be able to do again. These lists include the fundamental joys of my life: teaching and speaking to occasional audiences I value, such as the Trinity alums and the guests at the annual Book and Author Luncheon fund-raiser for the Cancer Therapy and Research Center. Somehow being unable to walk around the Park Ridge loop where I live or gallop along briskly on a treadmill don't make my list of regrettable losses.

But suddenly, without warning, I sleep through the night, and although still coughing occasionally, I am not gasping for breath. I am able to do my morning chores of cleaning litter boxes and filling bird feeders without taking breaks.

I rejoice. I say prayers of gratitude. I forage in my briefcase for materials I'll use in planning my spring semester syllabi, and I vow that the next time I feel puny I will think positively, look forward to recovery, and be, as I am always advising friends to be, a "patient" patient.

I want to believe I am capable of perseverance and fortitude in matters of health, but hypochondria, self-pity, and despair seem much easier.

The First Amendment

I reside in the usually gloriously beautiful Texas Hill Country, where wildflowers flourish; deer, sheep, goats, and even alpacas gambol; gorgeous avians—bluebirds, hummingbirds, barn swallows, cardinals, and even occasional blue herons (these perch patiently on the edge of my cistern waiting for an unwary koi to make the mistake of coming up for air) and swooping, chatty purple martins—fill the skies.

Not much of any of this occurred during this long, hot, dry summer. Instead of spending my allowance on fancy clothes, fine jewelry, or first editions of classics, I now suspect I have part ownership in Johnny's Feed Store. Every week I lug home fifty-pound bags of nourishing pellets for deer and expensive black oil sunflower seed for birds and squirrels.

And, of course, though I have "my own well" and am fretting constantly about running out of water, I learned to conserve carefully so that I could fill tubs and bowls with cool water to sustain the wildlife—even a family of black rock squirrels on my front porch, who reimbursed me for my investment by performing acrobatics to entertain my cats who sat transfixed at the windows. Were the cats admiring the cute squirrels or plotting ways to enjoy them as a snack? I don't want to know.

In spite of my desire to rant about the challenges of the drought and the fear that this summer is just a foreboding of droughts to come—remember Margaret Atwood's dreadful line in *Oryx and Crake*, "Texas had finally just dried up and blown away"?—I have always been intimated by authority. (I always comply with "No spitting on the floor" signs, for example.) When the editor told me that this was First Amendment Week and asked me to comment on that, I knew I must.

When I was an undergraduate, the guarantees of freedom of speech, assembly, religion, press, and petition seemed simpler. As a leader of student government and then during my early years as a student life administrator, one of the "adults in charge," I didn't really believe that students had any rights. They weren't full citizens, so formulating rules and ignoring due process were easy.

With rules we often simply inserted the adverb "appropriately" or "responsibly" to define conduct expected. And, of course, administrative staff determined the meanings of these words in areas ranging from attire on and off campus to articles published in the student-edited press, and even exhibitions featuring student art.

We endeavored to prevent loud noise and parties in the dorms by setting an arbitrary number of persons who could gather in a room. More than twelve, I think, was "inappropriate."

Were these the good old days? I think not, if you care about and respect the First Amendment. Eventually, campus administrators began to realize that although a university is not a democracy in which everyone has an equal vote, the academic community still needed to recognize that students were, big surprise, human beings and deserved to enjoy rights as well as to accept responsibilities.

Lately, however, I fear that I may be reverting. I catch myself yearning for some propriety and appropriateness. I've begun to question my father's admonition that has long guided my life—"You are as good as anyone but better than no one." I've begun to condescend and to disapprove of the manner in which some others exercise their rights.

I am wavering and sometimes think I am, in fact, better than some others. These others not only disregard what's "appropriate" or "responsible," they go so far as to cheer the mention of the number of executed inmates in Texas, as well as to applaud the momentary hesitation of a presidential candidate when asked if he'd let a critically ill thirty-year-old die if that patient had chosen not to purchase health insurance and, most recently, to jeer a gay American soldier in Iraq when he asked a question.

I can't stand to ask myself: If I truly support the freedom guaranteed in this amendment, how can I have the audacity to wish all citizens would use these freedoms more—here come those adverbs again—appropriately and responsibly, as I define those terms?

If these people call themselves Nazis, I would, perhaps, expect such absence of compassion, but I simply cannot bear thinking there is any truth in Bill Maher's recent
assertion that the term "Christian" these days means "people who hate charity and love killing."

Maybe part of the difficulty for me is that every
major religion I've ever read about or heard of has a significant commitment to compassion—has sacred texts that
admonish humankind to "do unto others as you would
have done to you."

What does any of this have to do with our First
Amendment rights? Well, it's just that I'm so appalled, dis-
gusted, and dismayed by the absence of compassion, by
the apparent loss of ability to listen to different perspectives, by the disrespect I find myself having for these people and their views, that I am a bit anxious about my own
commitment to these rights which I have for so very many
years considered precious. I'm troubled by thinking even
for a second that I'm better than another. I wasn't raised
that way.

I guess what I want is for those who have the blessing
of living in a society governed by such an amendment to
use our rights in ways that build community and develop
mutual respect. I guess I want Vonnegut's admonition
"You've got to be kind" to be understood and practiced as
a natural part of accepting the First Amendment. I guess
what I want is for humans to be compassionate, kind, considerate of all creatures—humankind and beyond—as well

as good stewards of this earth, as a prerequisite to their even having access to these rights.

Though it makes me queasy to admit it, I fear I'm yearning for "appropriately" and "responsibly" to be used once again to describe the conduct and behavior especially of those of us privileged to celebrate First Amendment rights. And it makes me even queasier to realize that many of you reading this are thinking, "She should have stuck with writing about the drought."

Although I did not compose this marvelous list (Sue Ellen Turner sent it to me in spring 2005), I feel I must include it in this collection since I read from it in every class I teach and need to reread it regularly in order to limit my frequent, inappropriate use of this particular word.

> When is *f@#$%** acceptable? Only ten times in history:
> 10. Capt. E. J. Smith of RMS *Titanic*, 1912: "What the f@#$%* do you mean, we're sinking?"
> 9. Mayor of Hiroshima, 1945: "What the f@#$%* was that?"
> 8. General Custer, 1877: "Where did all those f@#$%* Indians come from?"
> 7. Albert Einstein, 1938: "Any f@#$%*idiot could understand that!"
> 6. Picasso, 1926: "It does so f@#$%* look like her!"
> 5. Pythagoras, 126 BC: "How the f@#$%* did you work that out?"

4. Michelangelo, 1566: "You want *what* on the f@#$%* ceiling?"

3. Amelia Earhart, 1937: "Where the f@#$%* are we?"

2. Noah, 4314 BC: "Scattered f@#$%* showers, my ass!"

1. Saddam Hussein, 2003: "Jeez, I didn't think they'd get *this* f@#$%* mad!"

When I sent this list to Margaret Atwood on March 17, 2005, she added two more:

#11: "Where the @$%* did all the fresh water go?"

#12: "Why the @$%* can't I breathe?"

In spring 2015 Trinity student Leah Selznick added another:

#13: Anne Frank, 1943: "Who the @%&$* read my diary?"

On the Cusp of My Dotage

Bizarre coincidences abound. Just as I was reflecting on what I might focus on in an essay on aging, the ever thoughtful—maybe even prescient—folks at AARP published a disturbing piece in their online newsletter titled "9 Embarrassing Health Conditions and How to Treat Them."

Considering the audience for these distributions, I shouldn't have been so taken aback that these conditions ranged from smelly feet to frequent incontinence to uncontrolled flatulence. I could not, however, avoid being astonished by realizing that I deal with several of these embarrassments. Luckily, the ones that seemed most horrific have not yet afflicted me; most of these deal with the intestinal tract or dentures. That I've not experienced these problems yet is hardly comforting.

Recently, I've dragged both undergraduates and older students through discussions of Gary Shteyngart's slit-your-wrists satire *Super Sad True Love Story*.

His characters seek "life extension" through technology, and the resulting condition is not ideal. My students, of course, haven't yet recovered from Margaret Atwood's commentary on our generation's obsessions with physical appearances and extended lifetimes in *The Year of the Flood*, with the AnooYoo health spa, the gentlemen's club, Scales and Tails, and dancers wearing Biofilm Bodygloves.

In these and other contemporary novels, wise writers explore the heartbreaking and ridiculous lust for perfect bodies and eternal youth, yet many people keep hoping against hope.

I think I first spotted the aging process in myself in a dressing room, probably at Dillard's, when I had to send the helpful saleslady back out for a larger size. For decades, I have comfortably worn size 10, but somehow that era had ended. The Chico ensemble, with its elastic waistline, soft, flowing fabrics, and complicated sizing numbers that drew my mind off extra-large and plus sizes, quickly became appealing. (Brilliant marketing!)

Through careful selection of my wardrobe, I think, at the very least, I avoid repelling others by my "middle-age spread," even as I have moved far beyond that demographic. But in spite of avoidance, sometimes I can't help but see my full image, unclothed, in the bathroom mirror, and I almost always wonder who that fat lady with the droopy abdomen is. The flappy underarms still amuse me because of my idol, Bette Midler, drumming on hers and asking, "Don't you just hate it when your body gets a mind of its own?"

Alas, Chico's doesn't sell bathing suits, so that annual shopping experience has become particularly grueling and depressing. In addition to my weight gain and the shifting of my curves to places where one would just as soon not have a curve, the mirrors in dressing rooms convert mysteriously into brilliantly lit torturous reflections of strangers. For a while I tried suits with skirts, but the hems just flapped loudly in the shoreline breeze, attracting eyes. A modest suit and a sweeping, smothering cover-up gets me to and from the car.

Goodness knows, changes in physical appearance should not and do not obsess me; I, in fact, feel sorry for women who long benefited from meeting society's standard of "beauty." Aging must be horrific for them. I long ago realized that not having high cheekbones or a pert nose eliminated me from that category, but I have always had "good hair," and my gratitude for that is readily recognized when anyone notices that I've had the very same haircut (monthly) for several decades. Don't mess with a good thing.

Other than my hair, I've always liked my hands—long, slender fingers, smooth skin, expressive when I talk or lecture. Now they are the gnarled fingers found on the creepy villains of detective novels! When I attempt to point out an error in grammar or punctuation on a student's paper, the poor young adult can't find said error because the tip of my index finger is resting far from the intended target. And my days of making "rabbit ears" behind the head of an unsuspecting colleague in the group photo of department members are over; whoever saw a rabbit with her two ears leaning crookedly toward one another?

Beyond the distracting gnarled digits, they also aren't as trustworthy at holding onto pills or opening jars as they once were. Putting everything in perspective as is my wont, I recall a discussion with the late doctor Anne Farrell, who examined my fingers, asked, "Do they hurt?" and, when I replied no, responded, "Don't worry about it." (Now that that wonderful woman is gone, they do hurt occasionally.)

Nora Ephron wrote wonderfully about the necks of aging women in *I Feel Bad about My Neck, and Other Thoughts on Being a Woman.* "There are chicken necks. There are turkey gobbler necks. There are elephant necks. There are necks with wattles and necks with creases that are on the verge of becoming wattles." She quotes her dermatologist as stating that "the neck starts to go at forty-three, and that's that." As Ephron notes, no matter what cosmetics or collagen treatments you use on your face, the neck is a dead giveaway. "Our faces are lies and our necks are the truth."

Mine is an elephant neck, but some days I think I perceive some progress toward wattles. I don't much like the resemblance to the elephant, but for some vain reason, I like it better than a turkey. I've shied away from turkey images ever since I read what I consider the greatest comparison ever—Sylvia Plath's "turkey neck and turkey gizzards." Let's accept the blessing of an elephant neck, folds and all.

These physical inevitabilities of aging, then, do not oppress me, and, so long as I feel well and haven't been presented with any serious diagnosis *yet*, I try not to complain about changes in any body parts. I swear by Woody Allen's belief that the most beautiful words in the language aren't "I love you" but "It's benign."

I memorize the AARP listing of "embarrassing" afflictions and promise myself I will seek professional help when I develop them. I stand ready to deal with them ASAP.

Still, I can't help but wonder which most of us fret more about—embarrassing ourselves or growing older.

Sometimes I wish I could roller-skate up and down my long drive on "garbage can to the curb" days. Heavy breathing is nowhere near as much fun to do as it once was to read about when some romance writer described it to the oblivious adolescent me, with my perfect 10 body, bouffant hair, long, smooth fingers, and taut neck.

Coleen Grissom is a professor of English at Trinity University and the author of *A Novel Approach to Life*. A faculty member at Trinity for more than fifty years, she has received "honorary alumna" status and a scholarship in her honor. As dean of students and later vice president for student affairs, she has mentored, counseled, and influenced the lives of thousands of students. Though still teaching full time at Trinity and leading discussions of contemporary fiction in two literary excursions for "more mature" students, she resides in the Texas Hill Country, where her toy poodles, a rescued schnauzer stray, and her indoor cats enslave her.